My Mother-in-law Misadventures

Vincent Bernhardt

ISBN: 1940275024

ISBN-13: 978-1940275024

Published by Undefined Logic, LLC

First Printing: May, 2013

DEDICATION

I'm very thankful for all the people who helped me with this book, by reading it or by encouraging me. I apologize in advance if I don't thank you specifically.

Of course, a huge thanks to my Darling wife. Without her cheerful prompting and corrections I never would have finished this book. Thanks to my children, with special thanks to Elizabeth for the enlightening chapter she wrote and a hearty thanks to John, who very kindly provided me with excellent edits and a workable draft cover. Thanks to our brothers and their families for their support and encouragement (especially to Arlo and Barry). Thanks to Pastor Sonny and his lovely wife Gilly for the initial encouragement. Thanks to Jaki Broussard Rivon, a talented and published poet, for her kind words and recommendations. She means the world to us. (You should go buy her books!) Thanks to my friends who read the rough drafts and provided me with kind words and smiles: Colleen, Wes, Diana, Julie and Harry. Finally, thanks to James Altucher for the insights on his blog which made me imagine this book was possible.

The greatest thanks of all to the Everlasting God and Father who loves me even when I don't deserve it. May everything I do and write bring Him glory.

If you liked My Mother-in-Law Misadventures you might like some of the posts on my blog site (www.o-dark-thirty.blogspot.com), a few of which are directly related to this book (look for the tag *The Frau Chronicles*).

Discover other titles by Vincent Bernhardt:

Preparing for the Fiscal Cliff (with Marcella Bernhardt)

Contents

Greetings!

Thank you for purchasing The Frau Chronicles. I hope you enjoy the journey!

Would you please take a few minutes and write a review? I would appreciate it, and it gives other potential readers the correct guidance for purchasing the book. Please be nice, but certainly be honest.

Preface: The Main Characters

I am an ordinary guy. If you walked past me on the street you wouldn't notice me. These are stories of part of my life - some of the funnier parts. Who knew having a mother-in-law in the house with you could be so funny?

This isn't the story of my wife, though she appears in almost all of them. Darling, as I refer to her, is exactly that - she is a darling to me and a blessing to everyone who knows her.

Darling and I met at grief counseling sessions at our church, when we were both broken-hearted. You've been there, so you know what I mean. We weren't looking for love, yet we found it in each other.

Within a few months of our marriage her aged mother needed surgery and came to live with us. At seventy-five years old, she wasn't pleased with Darling's new husband and made that abundantly clear. When I referred to her as "Mom" she immediately corrected me, informing me in her heavy German accent that she wasn't my Mother. From that moment on I referred to her as "Frau" which is polite German for "Mrs."

Her short visit with us lasted over ten years. She and I endured each other. Trying to retain my sanity I started to journal the incidents that stretched my patience, keeping them under a working title of "The Frau Chronicles." Many of those stories appear here exactly as originally written. Some were funny. Some were angry. Some stories were simply written because of my total inability to understand this strange, happy, melancholy, sad yet sometimes amazing woman who lived under my roof.

Well, she thought I lived under her roof, which was another of those frustrating little things…

Yet for all the years we spent together I knew almost nothing of Frau's early years. Frau was born in Poland and married at the young age of nineteen to a man eighteen years older than she was. She and her new husband left all his wealth and position and fled World War II Nazi soldiers, eventually coming to the USA. She told anecdotal stories of these times while she lived with us, and we pieced together other parts of her younger years from documents she kept for half a century.

As I gathered my personal stories together, Darling and I also tried to piece together the mystery of her Mother's earlier years. To understand the present, you must understand the past. I lived with the woman for over a decade and she still baffled me. Meet her in these stories and share in the adventure.

On Frau and Intuition

Darling and I are sitting on the couch, each of us logged into the same on-line game on separate computers. We're on flying mounts gathering herbs and ore. The television is on; we play the game without sound and listen to our movie at just enough volume to hear it, but not quite enough to drown out the other television, the one on the other side of the living room wall - the television in the downstairs Master Suite.

Frau ambles out of her room, a few feet into the living room and sits on the love seat facing us, hands crossed in her lap, a small kerchief in her fist. Her grey hair is still put up on her head, even though it is close to eight in the evening. Her grey hair is tightly layered, neatly arranged in an old-style bun. I don't know how many hairpins she uses, but I find them occasionally on the living room or kitchen floor, a small orphaned metal shape missing its brethren. I just put them on the counter and they disappear, presumably restored to the hairpin family.

Frau is gasping a little, trying to catch her breath. We give her a minute. She is pale, but that's normal. After this many years I recognize when Frau is too pale, and she isn't. She's fine, and her red lipstick is perfectly in place. This means she recently put it on again, or that she hasn't been munching on the chocolate bars so carefully hidden in her room. She isn't wearing her glasses, so it's a planned visit, not a spontaneous journey from her reading chair to the living room. She is wearing her red dress with velvet slippers on her tiny feet. She sits and watches quietly until Darling looks at her with a wan smile. I heard today was a long day with Frau. I remain mute.

Frau's small fist is twisting a kerchief which was once white but now is a creamy color. The kerchief is cloth, with a bit of lace around the edges. I have no idea how old it is, but since Frau keeps everything this one could be from Noah's Ark. "Can you help me get something off my shelf?"she says to Darling. She speaks very firmly, each word carefully spoken. A heavy German accent colors all her words.

"Sure, Mom. Just a sec." Frau struggles to her feet and turns counter-clockwise, heading for her bedroom door. Darling closes her eyes briefly and sighs, then stands up tiredly. Darling goes through the archway and follows her mother into what I consider the Forbidden Sanctum, Frau's suite, the master bedroom of our house.

Off they go. From the muffled voices I know they've moved from the main bedroom into the bathroom and probably into one of the large closets. I try not to listen. Okay, I don't try not to, but I'm never really sure I want to. I hear "What do you mean, Mother? You can't even walk to the front door!" I don't hear the response, though I can detect there is a reply. A muffled sound, a few seconds pass and Darling comes out of the room, jaw clenched. Whatever the issue, it has Darling concerned. "Fine," she says over her shoulder and closes the door.

We need to close the door. There is fifty-year old mold in there that wants nothing better than to creep into the rest of the house and invade our lungs, seep into our furniture and put a patina of ancient mold spores on everything we own. The mold came into the house with Frau, and she doesn't even notice it. Frau and the mold were roommates for decades in her house in downtown Houston. When she moved in with us permanently eight years previously the mold came with her. I think it was lonely.

Darling sits down on the couch, her lips tight. I hesitate, but have to ask. "What's going on?" My paladin is already stored away and I've logged off the game.

"Mother wanted me to get her suitcase down for her. She says she's going on a trip and needs to pack." Her mage gracefully rises into the sky on an ebony dragon, searching for more ore in a fantasy landscape.

My mind races and I consider all the places that Frau could possibly visit. I know she wants to visit relatives in Germany again. She's been to Egypt and Israel. She enjoys telling the story of floating in the Dead Sea. She'd probably like France, and I can see her sipping different wine vintages. Ah, I think, she's off to Switzerland. She's tired of smuggling candy bars into her room and she's going for the real thing. Off to the chocolate capital of the world to indulge. I get a mental image of Frau sitting at a small Swiss bistro. Her red dress is spotless, with a large white napkin tucked under her chin. Her tiny hands are wrapped around a hot cup of cafe mocha. Chocolate éclairs surround her, and small chocolate candies occupy a dozen plates on the table in front of her. I can see the smudged chocolate on her lips, her eyes glistening with joy - or a sugar coma.

Then I realize the flaw in my vision. At this point in her life it would require a non-ambulatory destination. Perhaps she is planning an extended visit to one of Darling's four brothers here in Texas, but that's a more remote possibility than the trip to Switzerland. I cannot think of any practical locations. I give up guessing and raise an eyebrow. "Really? Where's she going?"

"She says she doesn't know, but she needs to get ready."

"Ah." I reply. I'm a little disappointed. Dutiful and loving husband that I am I have to add "Is her passport up to date?"

On Frau and Her House

Though I don't remember the first time I met Darling's mother, I do recall the first time I went to where she lived downtown. Frau was on a trip to Germany to visit relatives. Darling wanted to surprise her mom and do some house cleaning and I offered to help.

It was a hot summer day, and in Houston that would be in the high 90s. Built in 1907, the two-story house was close to a hundred years old and had once been the residence of Texas Governor Price Daniel when he was young. The house was built up off the ground, on blocks, which in the Houston area is not such a bad idea. Something failed in the structure and two corners were sagging, creating a slight break diagonally through the entire home. Time struck the house heavily and the aged structure was no longer a beautiful dwelling.

The house had gas lights when they first moved into it. Darling's father enclosed the front porch when she was a young girl. A huge old wooden desk dominated one side of the porch, hidden beneath stacks of books. Bookcases lined the walls, filled to bursting with volumes of various descriptions and categories. Now I'm a big fan of books, but these were not faring well in the environment, most of them disintegrating to uselessness.

Once through the old wooden door, previously the outside front door of the house, you entered the living room. Standing there you could look the length of the house, through the living room, into the dining area and then into the small kitchen toward the back part of the first floor. On the right side were windows with thick curtains, a small, heavy television, and a fireplace just at the intersection of the living room and the dining area.

The air in the house wasn't good. The combined smell of mold and mildew invaded everything. The heavy old-style curtains exuded toxic, aged vapors into the living room. After a few hours in the house neither Darling nor I could breathe well.

The focal point in the living room was a small chair with stuffed cushions, free of clutter, facing the little television, and flanked by two small tables covered with things: letters, open books, papers. I get that. My desk looks similar. A relatively nice couch sat against the wall opposite a matching love seat. Darling bought the newer items for her Mother a few months previous to our visit. Dust motes floated over the couch in a beam of sunlight. Knick-knacks sat everywhere, reminders, no doubt, of adventures past. A huge oil painting hung over the wood-burning fireplace, blackened with age and exposure to weather and soot. Fierce lions stared from that painting directly toward the chair.

The first door to the left went into the master bedroom, and another door led to the stairs to the second floor. I didn't venture toward the bedroom. For one thing, that's private and I already felt like an intruder. That was the room where Frau slept. For another, there was a bathroom off that bedroom, and I knew there was a current conflict with possums in there. A hole in the bathroom floor allowed them access, though I suppose Frau had it blocked somehow. I was pretty sure the possums would see me as the invader, with some justification.

I never saw the upstairs. That door to the upstairs only opened a crack, blocked from the other side by items fallen down the stairs. I have no idea what was up there. Books, souvenirs, trinkets, knick-knacks and families of small animals. Again, the strong smell of mold and mildew wafted toward us from the doorway.

Sweat poured from both of us after just a few minutes in the heat in the house. We straightened the living room and moved through the dining area. The table was covered with a tablecloth, which was barely visible under the dozens of items. An antique knife and fork set sat on one end. Many of the items in the room were entirely unfamiliar to me. It had been a while since that room had hosted any visitors.

Darling's cleaning plan centered on the kitchen. Her father made all the kitchen cabinets by hand and each showed the care of a true craftsman. We tackled some pots and pans and some errant dishes. When we finally finished, the kitchen counters sparkled and the cabinets shined.

So I don't remember when I met Frau, but I do recall how angry she was with Darling that she let me in the house, even to help clean. They didn't speak for weeks. By that time she was angry that Darling planned to marry me.

According to Frau, Darling needed a new husband with three attributes: 1) a widower, 2) grown children and 3) independently wealthy. So my relationship with Frau started with three strikes against me. She didn't start out as my biggest fan.

That changed a little over the years, but not much.

On Frau and Life with Us

Short months after our marriage in early spring, Darling learned her widowed Mother needed surgery. Darling knew that her mother had difficulty getting up and down, and often could do so only with great pain. The Doctors determined Frau needed a hip replaced, which Frau agreed to only because she could barely walk. When the Doctors prepared her for the hip surgery they also discovered some minor heart attacks, so she needed open-heart surgery.

Darling decided her Mother needed to come live with us and I agreed. We had a cute little house with three bedrooms. We had the Master Suite. Our house was not too big, but not too small and it sat on a nice corner lot. Frau moved into one small bedroom. We moved my two youngest children into the other bedroom and gave them bunk beds. Since they were with us only on alternating weekends, this seemed a small hardship. After all, this was only temporary.

By the time Frau recovered from her surgeries it was the middle of the summer. Her old house downtown had a single air conditioner in the window in the dining area which she used only during extremely hot months when Darling's father was ill, decades earlier. Her house had no modern energy-saving conveniences, so in the middle of a Houston summer it became a sauna without an air conditioner.

Darling convinced Frau she couldn't go back to her older, broken and roasting home. I think the few weeks with us in the cool air-conditioned interior of a modern home swayed Frau's opinion a little toward Darling's point of view.

About this time Frau needed carpal tunnel surgery on each hand, so the recovery period was extended a few months.

Darling and Frau started house hunting. They looked at a lot of houses and even thought of bidding on one of them. It was nice, with an upstairs master and a nice bedroom downstairs for Frau. That just wasn't going to work for her, apparently.

The houses that were acceptable to Frau were unacceptable to me, usually because of the location but sometimes just because I thought they were ugly. The few houses I liked did not appeal to Frau. Since we couldn't seem to reach a compromise, Darling quit hunting for a house. I was content thinking Frau would move back into her old home, broken as it was, at the end of the summer. Frau was vocal about her desire to move back also, but the house was an oven in the Houston summer weather. Darling cried when she thought of her Mother going back into that environment. I patiently waited for autumn.

One Saturday morning, Darling and her Mother went to a garage sale in a local neighborhood and noticed a sign for a house for sale. A nice house. A big house with a pool and on a cul-de-sac, both attributes I wanted. They talked to the owners and gave them a hundred dollars earnest money for a $200K house. Then they called me to look. When I got the call I knew this was the house - intuition, if you like. Impending doom sometimes does that.

This house had a nice Master Suite downstairs with a beautiful bathroom, whirlpool tub, and two huge walk-in closets. The Master also had a window/cubby thing that overlooked the koi pond which was in a small garden area. This little garden was also fenced off to help alleviate the noise from the nearby road. The location was the only drawback in my mind. The back of the house was against a major road through town, though there was a city-installed sound wall. The Master Suite was lovely and I really liked the wooden and tiled floors throughout the downstairs of the house. Alas, I might like the Master Suite, but...

Frau could not navigate stairs, so she moved into the Master Suite. It took months for Darling and her brothers to sort and move Frau's possessions from her downtown house. Some of it moved with Frau but much of it went to whichever brother wanted it and was willing to cart it off. Frau converted a third of our downstairs, the entire Master Suite, into a small microcosm of what she had in her house, with almost as much living area and free space, I think.

We got? A small bedroom upstairs - the one with the door to part of the attic. I crammed my clothes into half the tiny closet. Darling put some of her clothes in there and the rest in the game room/study out in the hall. We shared a little bathroom at one end of the upstairs hallway. Our new room in this large house was big enough for our bed, two nightstands, one large dresser and one standing dresser, with a small make-up table. You didn't want to turn around fast or take the corner too tightly or you scraped your side or back on the edge of the dresser at the doorway.

Each of the two younger children had their own room - larger than ours, actually. They shared the two-sink bathroom at the opposite end of the upstairs hallway. We had an empty bedroom upstairs we used for storage and a narrow study for my desk.

On the bright side, I knew I could do pretty much anything I liked while I was upstairs; Frau couldn't climb those stairs to save a life. On the dim side, the house had an open architecture and I really couldn't wander around in my underwear or anything.

Temporary was going to last for over a decade.

On Frau and the Lass

This addition to the book was penned by my very talented daughter, the Lass, also a writer.

When I first met Grandma, we were in the car. While Mom went to lock the house, her mother, a strange round-faced woman, pivoted in the front seat of the car and held out her hand.

"Hello," I said, my voice all small. "It's nice to meet you." I shook her hand, like I'd been taught.

She nodded in approval, jerked my hand up and down twice in her firm grip, and said, "Good! You have a strong grip!" She turned to my brother and repeated the procedure. Her eyebrows shot up, brushing her hairline. Her eyes grew wide, and she pursed her lips together an instant before grinning. "You too?" she said, and began to laugh, a big, hiccupping, belly-shaking laugh.

I laughed, too, though mine was more of a shy hiccup. She had sounded so surprised that both of our grips were strong, and her eyes had gotten so big so fast! She whooped again and again. My brother and I glanced at each other. I hoped I wasn't the only one worried. Mom had said Grandma couldn't breathe well, not to tire her out...was this tiring her out? What if she stopped breathing?

Just when I started to worry, Grandma's laughs subsided to a lower chuckle. "No-yah," she said in a thick accent, "you must have a good STRONG grip." She grabbed my hand again, tightly, in hers. "Know why?"

"No," I said, my eyes wide. "Why?"

She swung my hand lightly as she talked, back and forth and up and down, fist slowly clenching tighter. "If you meet someone, and they shake your hand, and you have good STRONG grip" -- she switches grips to my brother's hand now -- "then they know that you are trustworthy, a GOOD man! Like your papa," she said. "He is a good man. Does he have a good grip?"

My brother and I nod.

"Well, there you go!" She nodded. "From him you get your handshake."

My Mother-in-law Misadventures

Mom came back and we drove across town, moving from Grandma's ramshackle house in Houston to our own house. When we went inside, my brother and I hovered in the living room. Instructed in the true ways of Southern hospitality, we knew there would be no video games or ramblings with a guest here. Eventually, I sat by Grandma on the couch, listening to her stories. I don't remember the stories. I only remember one.

"Do you know the Ten Commandments?" she asked me suddenly.

I nodded. My dad made us go through them every night, mentally marking which ones we'd broken so we could apologize for them in our family prayers.

"You do?" Again, her eyes grew wide and filled with wonder, and she laughed. "What are they?"

I stood up. I was about nine or ten and had learned to stand when reciting memorized things. Then I recited them, King James style, full of thous and shalt nots.

When I finished, she rocked with laughter again, clapping her hands together slowly. Kids at school slow-clapped when they were being sarcastic, but not Grandma. She brought her hands a few inches apart between each clap, then pounded them together with a vigorous, echoing clash.

"I don't believe it!" she said. "You know the Ten Commandments!"

"It's not that big a deal. My brother knows them, too," I said, abashed.

"He does?" Her eyes widened. "Can he say them?"

"Sure." I turned to my brother, who sat a little ways away.

He wandered over. Once he understood that Grandma wanted him, too, to say the Ten Commandments, he echoed my previous recitation. Our voices rose and fell in the same places; we both paused before the sixth one, unsure whether to say "adultery" or "kill" first, and then corrected ourselves. But he, too, finished flawlessly.

Again, Grandma laughed and clapped. "Where is my purse?" she said to my brother. "Do you know where it is?"

"Here it is," I said, and fetched it from the other side of the couch. "Here you go, Grandma. Do you need help finding something?"

And then she told us the story.

"When I was a teacher in the refugee camp, I said I'd give one hundred dollars to any one of my students who knew the Ten Commandments. And now, I've found two!"

She gave us both a hundred dollars, despite our incredulous protests. We told her it didn't matter, us knowing the Ten Commandments, that it truly wasn't anything special. Most kids at our previous Christian school had known them. But like our handshakes, Grandma would not believe this made us anything less than extraordinary.

Over the years, she never stopped being impressed by that moment. "You are GOOD kids," she'd say to me. "You listen, you know the Ten Commandments..."

Occasionally, in the midst of a different conversation, Grandma would pause and say, "Your papa, yes, he is a GOOD man. He knows the Lord, he teaches you the Ten Commandments..." This statement was always followed with an approving head nod.

My dad took the money and put it in bank accounts for us. I knew it was in the bank. As the years went by, I knew that saying Bible verses had earned me enough money to buy the world - a world that Grandma, with her long laugh and slowly clapping hands, never ceased to find amazing.

On Frau and Bruises

I came down the stairs one bright, summer Saturday morning rubbing my sleepy eyes and ready to clean the pool. I wasn't the first one up. Darling had been up and around for over an hour and Frau was certainly awake. Frau didn't seem to sleep as much as I did, though she caught a lot of naps during the day, usually with her television going at full volume.

I was halfway down the stairs before my brain registered the scene in the living room. Frau sat on the couch in her flannel nightgown, purple velvet slippers tucked firmly on her tiny feet, the seat reclined as far as it could go. Her chubby little left hand was holding a towel with an ice pack over the left side of her face, the side facing me.

Darling was nowhere to be found, but the door to Frau's room was open.

When we first moved into the house, Frau moved into the Master Suite downstairs. She had plenty of room, a nice downstairs bathroom with a whirlpool tub and not one, but two master closets. She filled them both to overflowing, clothes packed as tightly together as clowns in a circus car. Shortly after we moved into the house Frau indignantly proclaimed, quite loudly, that someone went into her room and stole change from her money jar. Since the only people in the house at the time were Darling and I and my two youngest children, I took offense at the accusations. I vowed never to go into her room unless I had a specific task and an escort. I made my two youngest children promise the same thing. Frau had a keyed, locking doorknob installed on her room. Whenever she left the house, she locked the room and took the key.

I stood on the bottom step of the staircase and pondered my next move. I could quietly exit through the kitchen and Frau wouldn't hear me, and I could then clean the pool in the warmth and relative quiet of the summer morning.

Yeah, I couldn't do that. A better course of action decided upon, I moved next to Frau on her right side and sat on the (very sturdy) coffee table. She didn't see me, and since I'm as quiet as my stealthy

Native American ancestors she didn't hear me either. Okay, it helps that Frau is mostly deaf. Frau's right eye was closed, but I could see the bruise on the left side of her face. "Hey," I said, at medium volume. The cat jumped and ran from the room. "You okay?"

"No, no. I'm good." She opened her right eye and looked at me, even managing a tremulous smile. "God takes care of me. My daughter is helping me."

"Okay," I replied, standing. "Just thought I'd check." My duty discharged, I was ready to quietly clean the pool and avoid the current drama.

Darling appeared at Frau's bedroom door and I went to her. I whispered, sure that Frau could not hear me. "What happened? Did she fall?" Frau could be frustrating, so I tried to ease the situation with humor. I lowered my voice even further and asked quietly. "Did you get fed up and clobber her?"

Darling looked at me like I lost my mind and just shook her head. "She has a black eye. When I woke her up I noticed it, so I brought her out here and put some ice on it." Darling looked concerned. "I don't see anything knocked over in her room. Everything looks okay. She was in bed when I found her and I don't think she fell into anything. She says she doesn't know what happened and doesn't remember falling."

"She seems okay. How bad is it?"

"Well, it's just a black eye and she'll be fine. If I thought she fell, that would be a different story, but she's all right."

"God takes care of me." Frau's voice interrupted us. I never can tell what she can hear and what she can't. She scares me a little that way.

If Frau actually fell in the night, we'd hear her. After all, our room was right above Frau's and we could faintly hear the television in the middle of the night when Frau couldn't sleep, or when she slept with the television on.

I wasn't needed for anything so I went outside to clean the pool.

Summer heat comes early in the day in Houston, and our pool caught the full morning sun, shade from the house slowly stalking across the surface of the pool in mid-afternoon. Already on this Saturday morning the concrete around the pool was too hot to go barefoot. After doing the outside edges of the pool and cleaning the baskets I went back inside to get my swimsuit. That was the part of cleaning the pool that I liked, especially on sunny mornings.

Frau was no longer on the couch, and the door to her room was closed. Darling sat on the couch, her eyes closed.

"You okay?" I asked. She looked exhausted. Taking care of her mother is hard work.

Darling looked up at me with tears in her eyes and started laughing. "She doesn't want me to tell anyone, but it's too funny." Darling was gasping between bouts of laughter. I just stood in the middle of the living room like an idiot, totally confused. Darling wiped her eyes with a tissue. "Her teeth fell out last night. She went to bed with her teeth in and they fell out on her pillow. She rolled over in the middle of the night on her teeth. That's where she got the black eye."

Now that Frau had her teeth back in her mouth, her appetite returned and life resumed its accustomed pace. Darling added her mother's teeth to the list of things she needed to check as she helped Frau get into bed and settled each night. But we aren't always vigilant.

Another bright Saturday morning, a few weeks later, I noticed that Frau was limping slightly as she moved slowly from the kitchen table to her room. Her appetite was certainly fine for breakfast that day, but she pushed her walker step by step more slowly in front of her than usual.

"She okay?" I asked Darling when we were alone again, listening to Frau's television start up after she shut the door.

Darling didn't burst into laughter this time, but she smiled. "Well, I forgot about her teeth last night and she went to sleep with them in her mouth." I shrugged, still not clear. "I found them a bit further in her bed this morning. Mom's a little … bruised." Darling patted her left hip area.

"Are you kidding me? You're telling me … she bit her own butt?"

This time I was the one who couldn't stop laughing.

On Frau and Groceries (and the Original Argument)

Groceries and bills were a big topic early on. Darling would come into the house with groceries, and I helped get them to the kitchen. Frau usually wandered off to her suite with a few plastic bags. A raised eyebrow elicited the response from Darling "It's mostly just fruits."

Okay, well, I'm not too keen on food being stored in the rooms, but I don't go into Frau's room. I guess it shouldn't matter much to me. I know food is stored in there and sometimes I wonder how old it gets or does it get misplaced among the strewn items in the suite? Will we someday find bananas hidden under the chair, desiccated and moldy? Chocolate bars abandoned in the seat cushions? I shudder a little. Perhaps we'll find small animals munching on abandoned chips under her bed.

Some of this stems from my own childhood, of course. When I was a boy we went out for Halloween like most kids. I recall being so joyous over the free candy (a rare treat in my family) that I promptly set some of it aside and hid it under my mattress in a small paper bag, safely tucked away for a day when sugar was scarce and I needed access to my hidden trove. Now Halloween comes in the end of October. Sometime in the early spring, as my mother was flipping over my mattress during those horrid spring cleaning days, she discovered my personal and well-hidden cache of goodies. Though I don't think any of the candy was chocolate, it didn't matter. Mom had some choice words for me and the candy was lost to me forever. I had hidden all that candy and promptly forgotten about it. And I was young with a relatively good memory. Frau is certainly no longer young and her memory is questionable.

I haven't a clue how much food Frau stashes in her suite. I know she stores canned herring in there, since I see the cans occasionally appear in the trash can in the kitchen. Perhaps storing all that food is a good thing. If a hurricane runs through the region and we find ourselves short of food, perhaps she has stored enough to sustain us for a while. I do know she occasionally comes out of her room and simply picks at her dinner, or declines eating altogether (though that is certainly a rarity). I suspect those are the times Frau is hungry before dinner and she delves into her store of goodies in her room. And it isn't all fruit. She has chocolate in there, and it doesn't consist of the small bars either. Cheaper in bulk, so bulk it is! But I refused to have an argument with Frau over food in her room. We had our big arguments when she moved in, and I wanted no others.

Make no mistake, Frau had a mean streak in her. "Old people get that way," Darling told me. I disagreed. My Mother remained kind and good-natured as she aged. Frau was also stubborn, a trait we have in common. This, naturally, led to confrontations.

One of our early arguments about living in the house concerned the bills, especially after receiving the first month's electricity bill, which was over three hundred dollars.

"This should not be so." Frau was furious at the amount. Her lips were pressed together and her face was pale. "You should call them and have them do something about that bill."

"It is what it is." I was looking at Darling for help with that one, but she could only shrug. "I read the meter. It's all legit."

"You must have read it wrong." Frau sat at the table, the electric bill quivering in her fingers.

"I did not read it wrong. I know how to read a meter." The look she gave me indicated that she thought it was entirely possible I had no clue how to read an electric meter.

"This is too much. They need to make it smaller. When I lived in my other house I never paid more than six dollars for the electric." Frau was literally shaking her chubby little index finger at me. My head started to throb.

"Yes, yes, I know this, but this is not your other house." I have a bad tendency to imitate the speech cadence of other people. It isn't intentional. Now I was sounding like Frau, except for the accent.

"It is schlecht. It is wrong. You are wanting me to pay half of this?"

"I don't want you to pay any of it." Now I was losing my temper. My voice rose in volume. I clenched my teeth together.

"Oh, so I should just move back to my other house, is that what you are saying?" She stood up with some difficulty and huffed from the room shaking the electricity bill in her hand like a dog shakes a rat.

I threw my hands up in the air and retreated to the back yard to clean the pool again. Since I cleaned the pool when I was angry at the old woman, we had the cleanest pool in the neighborhood.

The entire topic of bills became such an issue in the first few months that I created an elaborate, full-color multi-page presentation in large fonts and wordlessly handed it to Frau after dinner one evening a few nights later.

Lips clamped tightly together, Frau stalked (as best she could) back to her room and closed the door.

My terms were simple. Darling and I were responsible for all the bills in the house. No more discussions. We'd buy the food, we'd pay the utilities, and we'd maintain the pool and the yard and the house. Since Frau didn't drive and had no car, her only expenses were her own whims. We required nothing from her. Frau was Darling's mother and it was our obligation (though I might have worded that as "privilege") to care for her.

We had another few discussions, somewhat less heated, where Darling assured her mother that she should live with us and we would take care of her. Each time Frau brought the presentation with her and each time ended with the statement that she "should move back to my other house."

Our pool sparkled.

Frau finally accepted the agreement and we had no more discussions about bills. As a matter of fact, to the best of my knowledge we never told her how much any of the bills were after that, which is a good thing. One very hot summer month our electric bill topped seven hundred dollars. Frau might have died of a heart attack over that one.

I wish it was only six dollars!

On Frau and the Tool Shed

Mere weeks after moving into the big house, Darling and I decided we needed a shed for our outdoor tools. The garage was (and remained) almost full of other items.

We picked a spot in the back yard under a huge fir tree to put the shed. The spot wasn't quite level, but it was packed earth from some of the gardening work done elsewhere in the back yard and it was the right size. We bought the ready-to-assemble kit for the shed and early one Saturday we started working on it.

A hot summer day, we at least had a breeze to cool us and the fir tree provided some shade. In Houston you don't get cool shade, but warm shade is acceptable.

We leveled the area with sand mixed with concrete. If there's a better way, please don't tell me about it now. It's the only way I knew how to do it. Tamp, tamp with a couple two-by-fours. Darling had one end and I had the other. Thump, thump with a landscape timber for some of the harder spots. That was my handiwork.

Somewhere during that time, Frau ambled out to sit in the lawn chair and watch us. She was quite good about it and never offered any advice to either of us. After a while we forgot she was there and she occasionally dozed off.

We growled putting that shed together. I snarled every time I pinched my finger or put something together backward. This is normal building behavior for me, so I was used to having to disassemble and reassemble. We sweated in the heat and drank gallons of icy water from the house.

Darling was calm and competent. When I reached a spot that seemed to give me trouble she provided solutions. Between the two of us we had the shed completed by late evening. A full day's work from ground pounding to completed structure! Tools stored, band-aids and smiles all around, and we went back in for the night. I'm sure we took a dip in the pool, too, but I don't remember doing so.

"You and your husband did good today," Frau told Darling later.

"What do you mean, Mom?" Darling was baffled.

"Your Poppa and I would have killed each other trying to work together building that shed."

She liked me better after we built that shed, I think. In later years Frau even told other relatives the story of how we built the shed together and didn't kill each other. From Frau, that was high praise.

I'll take it.

On Frau and Cable TV

Let's talk about cable TV. We changed services a few months ago. Another company was offering to put cable into four rooms for the same price we pay now.

Frau had a problem with the previous cable. She had a box in her room and a controller with about a million buttons on it, and inevitably she would change the TV station to non-cable. Sometimes she would mention to Darling that the TV picture wasn't very clear and Darling had to fix it, switching the television input from airwaves back to cable.

The new service had a remote control with fewer buttons. At first we had her room connected to the DVR box we have. That wasn't working. I'd look at the movies we recorded and there would be parts of news programs and it would be planning to record strange shows at odd hours. That part was a mess. Obviously the remote still had a few too many buttons and Frau was delightedly and unknowingly recording what she watched. The DVR controls had to go.

So we had the installation guys reconfigure the system. I won't go into the configuration problems but we ended up with two of our televisions, the one in the den and the one in the office, both in control of the DVR. This left Frau with basic cable and a control with a lot less buttons.

She still changed the television channels and lost cable. I bought a remote control with five buttons, but it was too small for her hands and she couldn't see the buttons. Plus I needed to voluntarily go into her room to program it. I shrugged it off. I did what I could and it's up to her to watch cable or change it to a snowy local channel.

Then her television broke. Now I don't know how old her TV was, but it decided that it was going to show her the very minimum picture available. It reduced the picture on the tube to a single white line across the middle. I was pretty sure this was no fault of Frau's and her remote had nothing to do with it. That TV was dead. It might have been the victim of the mold in the room. I didn't know, and it didn't matter.

Darling and I had a seldom-used TV in our room and we figured it would be a nice TV for Frau. Certainly it was better than one with a white line across the screen.

Darling and I went into Frau's room and I disconnected the old TV. That ancient television was just a bit too small for two people to carry and a bit too large to comfortably get my arms around it. And it weighed about, oh, two million pounds or something. Darling wanted me to wait until I could get the Lad to help me carry it, but I'm not a big fan of waiting. I put a hand under the opposite corners of this beast and staggered out to the side of the house, where I dropped it in anticipation of heavy trash day. Part of it broke when it hit the ground, but, frankly, I didn't care. I promised myself I would start going to the gym regularly. (I made the same promise when I lugged it to the curb on heavy trash day, by the way.)

So we set up the smaller television in Frau's room and, with some technical help, got the cable running again for her perusal.

Two days later Frau was watching her tiny TV in her bathroom since she wasn't getting a picture on the TV we brought down for her. It just didn't pull the local channels in as well as her old television, according to Frau. I'm baffled.

So last week Frau has Darling take her to one of the big stores close by and she plunks down a bit less than a grand on a new TV for her room. They deliver it, and carry ours back to our room upstairs, but it's my job to configure them both.

It's a nice TV, I have to say. Big forty-some inch flat panel, wide-screen. I can lift it with one hand while making the connections with the other. "Whoa," I say to Darling. "Did you know this baby has a computer connection? We could hook it up to one of the computers!" I guess I'm not immune to television envy.

I admit to being peeved that Frau wasn't too appreciative of the television we put in her room. I'm not sure why it bothers me so much. "It was broken," she says, but it's really a remote control problem.

So I get the new television hooked up and the nice lady from the cable company helped me figure out the control code so that the cable remote also controls the TV. "Too bad we can't disable the numbers for the control" I say after she helps me configure it.

"Well, we have a control code that disables everything for the television except the power and volume," she says to me. So that's the code I use and I try it out. No way can Frau accidentally change the channel on the new TV. She can only control the channels on the cable. Perfect.

"So my new television should have a control. Where's the control for my television?" she asks me the next day, as I am sitting in the living room.

"You don't need it," I reply. "It will change the wrong channels."

"Oh," she says and walks back into her room. Her lips are firmly set and she walks a bit stiffly, so I know she is angry about my response. I also know she is looking for the remote control, but I hid it in the same place that I put the special code for the cable remote. So far she is still on the cable stations.

Except she isn't happy about the new television. She had Darling try to change the picture so it filled the entire screen. "You don't want to do that." I say, sagely. "If you use wide-screen on a normal channel all the people will be really short and wide."

It occurred to me later that maybe that's what she wants.

Turns out, though, that the screen handles the picture just fine. Darling needed the TV remote to fix the ratio. And she let her mom have it back.

On Frau and the News

"And so did you see what the stock market did today?" Frau sat in her chair at the table, a napkin firmly tucked under her chin. I don't recall the meal, but I am confident that Frau's plate had a small potato on it. She rarely had a dinner without a potato.

We discussed the news as we ate. We talked about the stock market. We talked about how the government was trying to take the just earnings of hard-working people, but that latter was usually when tax time approached.

Frau was an expert on the news. Her television was rarely on a channel that did not cover world, national and local events. I knew this because the volume was loud enough for me to hear her television clearly from my living room couch if I focused. That was when she was in her room with the door closed.

Occasionally I would come home from work and Frau and Darling would be watching the news in the living room, comfortably seated on the couch, a cat curled up in each lap. Frau would be reclined, with her short legs almost reaching half-way to the foot rest. She never could get the reclined seat back upright without help. There just wasn't enough leverage for her to push the footrest back. Sometimes the news would be on, Darling would be perusing web sites on her computer and Frau would be sound asleep on the couch. If I turned the news off Frau would wake up. "Oh," she'd say, "I'll go into my room and watch the news."

I don't watch the news. I look over the headlines every day on a half dozen news web sites and read the ones that interest me. I think this method is efficient, even if it isn't very thorough.

So whenever she asked me if I watched the stock market or saw the news I'd respond "Yes." Then we'd talk about the market, and how it was up or down. We'd focus on my favorite stocks, or the ones that Frau took an interest in during the last ten hours of watching continuous news feeds over the airwaves. Inevitably I'd smile at her. "But you don't have money in the stock market," I'd say.

"Oh, this I know," she responded. "I tried the stock market one time and…" she launched into the story of a relative who talked her into making an investment and how all the money was lost in the stock market. You'd think after hearing it a dozen times I'd remember names and amounts, but I don't. Frau did, though. "So, of course I do not trust the stock market." That conversation always ended that way.

She was especially animated during election times and we had lively discussions of the merits of the candidates. She knew more about the candidates than I did, so those talks were always fascinating for me.

Frau and I rarely talked about political parties, though we both had some strong opinions and, strangely, we didn't disagree. We both focused on the candidates. It didn't take me very many election years to figure out how Frau chose to vote. She voted for the person who didn't threaten her Social Security and the ones who promised to take the least amount of money from her.

Unfortunately, they all made that same promise, regardless of party affiliation. Eventually her political choices boiled down to whichever candidate seemed most honest to her, according to all the news stations she watched. I'll just add, sometimes the mud-slinging advertisements backfired; Frau wasn't fond of politicians who didn't play nice, and I agreed with her.

Frau watched all the news with equal delight. She was more conversant with sports teams than I was, though we had some lively short talks about celebrities and the drama in Hollywood lives.

I think she was addicted to news. I don't even know if that's possible. If she went for more than a few hours without watching the news she was anxious to get back to her television. Occasionally she came into the living room and watched a movie with us, which delighted me, even though she inevitably dozed off before the end.

"So what happened?" she'd say as she awoke, a half hour after the movie was over. I'd then give her a brief summary of the ending and she would nod. "I'll go watch the news now," she'd say, then disappear to do just that.

Once in a while, though, she watched a movie in her room. She liked westerns and spy thrillers. I know this because I heard the show through the wall. If it sounded like a good movie I'd change the channel in the living room and watch the same show.

Not the news, though.

On Frau and the Koi Pond

The big house had everything we all wanted. I wanted a cul-de-sac home with a larger lot and a pool. Frau wanted a willow tree and a waterfall. No, really, she wanted a waterfall. Darling didn't even know that her Mother wanted one until a few months after we moved into the house, when Frau took an old magazine picture from her Bible and showed it to Darling. It was a colored picture of a small waterfall, the water gently cascading over rocks. Darling was delighted that her Mother had a waterfall visible from her room. She wanted her Mother to be happy, or at least content.

Okay, I wanted a big screen television, too, but I just moved the couch closer to our television.

A tiny garden area strategically sat outside the Master Suite, visible from the room's bay window. The small waterfall flowed into the koi pond over a nice cascade of reddish stone. We had thirteen koi fish and two turtles in that pond when we moved in. A year after we moved in we only had seven fish. I know this because Darling mentioned that the pond was dirty and needed cleaning. When she went on a weekend retreat I put on my grubbiest clothes and went out there on Saturday morning.

It took me a few minutes to catch the seven koi and a few more minutes to realize that our count was low and I wasn't going to find any others. Do turtles eat fish? Are we supposed to feed the koi? Were they cannibals? I had no idea. The koi pond is outside my normal range of surveillance and totally enclosed by a tall fence. The only way in or out is via one of the doorways from the enclosed sun room in the main house.

Just in case sushi is a turtle favorite I used a different bucket to hold the two turtles. I put some nice clean water in the bucket and tracked them down. After a brief search and grab, in the bucket they both went. At this point I was covered in mud and slime and other black stuff I probably didn't appreciate as much as I should. I also realized I had nothing to drink, so I drank from the hose. Hey, I'm a working man, thigh deep in brackish water! Of course I can drink from the hose.

The water did taste a little funny, though. I later recalled that the hose was often dropped into the pond to replenish the water level.

I moved some of the decorative rocks and used another bucket to slosh the murky water from the pond. At some point I realized Frau watched me from the window of her room, but I don't suffer from stage fright. I do well with an audience.

I scooped large handfuls of mud from the pond. Rinse with some water. Scoop with bucket. Scoop mud with hands. Repeat. I felt like a bad shampoo commercial. Lather, rinse, repeat.

When the pond was relatively clean I filled it with fresh water and sat on the edge for close to an hour while it warmed in the spring sunshine. Yes, I know it can harm the koi to toss them back in too early, but they weren't too happy about being in a bucket either. I waited until I was bored, then poured them back in. They immediately disappeared under the rocks I had carefully arranged for them. I didn't even get a thank-you for my architectural ingenuity.

The turtles were another story entirely. You'd have to see the bucket to understand. The bucket that once contained two turtles in pristine clear water from the hose was now inky black water. I pondered that a bit and thought of the last three hours cleaning the koi pond. I decided the turtles were to blame.

I moved both turtles to a local pond, where they enjoyed their new home and our koi fish enjoyed cleaner water.

I don't know if Frau appreciated the cleaner pond, but without turtles, we soon had water lilies and she loved those. Darling was delighted with the clean pond. She wasn't so happy about the dirty jeans and shirt.

I knew I should have ditched them with the turtles.

On Frau and Garage Sales

Frau loved to go to garage sales but I think it was to meet people, not to buy anything. She was always looking for a good deal, though. Darling said her mother didn't need to buy anything, but simply loved to look for good deals and thoroughly enjoyed haggling over the prices. Frau often talked the sellers down to her price.

Everyone seemed delighted by this small old woman looking at their garage sale items. She asked everyone she met "How old do you think I am?"

That's a trick question, by the way. The only way to win at that one is to guess lower than the person appears, but high enough that they think you are serious. Guys can get away with answering "You look about a hundred" if an old man asks this question.

With Frau there was very little chance of guessing her age correctly. In her mid-seventies when she came to live with us she easily looked ten years younger than she was. That never really changed; she always looked about ten years younger than she was, though it was probably ten years older than she thought.

I don't have many stories of going on garage sales with Frau. That was something that Darling did with her, and they both enjoyed themselves immensely. Quite often they would find some knick-knack or bric-a-brac to bring home and embellish our home, but not always. Frau always sought out and purchased broken jewelry, which she stored in one of her closets. Darling told me that her mother repaired old jewelry when she was younger and made necklaces from jewelry pieces. I guess Frau planned to return to that hobby, though I had no idea of her timeline to do so.

I'm not an expert at garage sales. One of the first times I met Darling she was having a garage sale at her house and I drove by. I wasn't doing anything that morning and since she was sitting by herself I asked if she wanted some help. She didn't know me well then, so she smiled and said "sure." I sat with her for a while and watched. I wasn't sure what I was supposed to be doing when people showed up. Mostly I figured I'd keep an eye out for the ones who pocketed small objects and then tackle them and hold them for law enforcement to book them for stealing a twenty cent item.

At one point during that garage sale Darling went in the house for a few minutes and left me in charge. I felt empowered. While she was absent I had at least five customers walk up and browse the items she had so carefully laid out on tables and put little price stickers on. (Darling takes her garage sale responsibilities quite seriously.) One lady shopper held up an item with a fifty-cent price tag "Would you take a quarter for this?" I pondered that at great length and after one point seven seconds I said "Sure." This created a mad rush of all the customers to bring me items and offer me half the listed price, which I cheerfully accepted. Darling, as it turns out, wasn't nearly as delighted with my newfound ability to move inventory and didn't leave me alone again for the next hour or so.

Darling also took our two youngest, the Lass and the Lad, on garage sale outings. Being a voracious book reader the Lass rarely found anything that interested her in garage sales, but Darling often brought me boxes of books to peruse from her solo forages into the "garage sailing" world.

The Lad, however, learned the lessons of negotiation from Darling, a master of garage sales. I didn't realize how well he learned the lessons until one bright Saturday morning when Darling and Frau were off doing something else. I decided to take the Lass and the Lad "garage sailing" myself. They exchanged puzzled glances and off we went, touring the nearby neighborhoods for items worthy of purchase.

Normally I don't see much of anything that interests me in garage sales. At the time, though, I thought it would be a good idea to set an example for my two youngest. The Lad was about six and I wanted to impress him with my abilities as a purveyor of exotic garage sale bargains. At one house I noticed a GPS device about the size of a paperback and with a green LCD screen. Color GPS devices weren't really available at the time. This one seemed like quite the bargain at only fifteen dollars, so I looked it over and set it back down, examining the other items on the tables.

A few minutes later I noticed the Lad turning the item over and studying it. "Hey," I said. "I was looking at that."

He just looked up at me and smiled. "It's still here."

"You don't have fifteen dollars," I responded, somewhat miffed. He shrugged and put it back down. Not wanting to miss out on such a desired bargain I promptly bought the GPS from the lady running the sale. When we got back in the car the Lad looked at me. "How much did you pay?"

Puzzled I simply looked at him. "Fifteen dollars," I said.

He shrugged and looked out the window. "I would have offered her ten." He was obviously annoyed with me that I got such a bargain.

We drove for a bit and I couldn't stand having a new toy and not using it. Pulling into a local church parking lot I pressed the buttons and got my new GPS up and running, but without the directions I couldn't figure out how to display my current coordinates. Frustrated I growled as I set it back down on the floor. "Should never have bought the thing," I mumbled.

The Lad glanced at it and looked over at me. "I'll give you five dollars for it."

He had it running by the time we got home. I never went to a garage sale with him again. Darling and Frau did, though.

On Frau and Hurricane Rita

Hurricane Rita blew into the Houston area in late September of 2005.

I didn't travel much with Frau, but Hurricane Rita gave me the chance to do so. After the landfall of Katrina in New Orleans a month earlier, everyone in the Houston area was cautious of Rita. We decided to evacuate to Dallas, where one of our daughters had a house. We gathered the cats and some key belongings and piled into the car. Frau sat in the back seat, next to the cats.

The four hour trip took us fourteen hours. Our eldest daughter made the same trip on the back roads in only six hours, but we didn't know that at the time. During the entire trip Frau never complained, but simply dozed and talked to Darling. We probably talked about the news and some celebrity gossip.

I don't have many good memories of the trip up there, and none of the trip back (which was entirely uneventful). The key point is that I also don't have any bad memories of the trip up. Along with three million other Houstonians we were captured in the tangled web of non-moving traffic on congested freeways leaving the city. Friends of mine had horror stories of running out of gas, of running out of water to drink, of being caught in the center of lanes of stationary vehicles. One friend told me of a harrowing encounter at a gas station with a man who had poor intentions toward her and a timely rescue by a stranger.

I don't have any of those stories. I remember the big dog on the truck next to us, who seemed to be enjoying the adventure, though I suspect a dozen hours in the back of the truck eventually wore him out also. I remember a dear friend calling me on my cell phone and warning me to leave the area while we were on the road. He lived in the New Orleans area during the Katrina landing. I remember Darling humming some tunes to the radio.

We made one stop to refuel the car and take a much-needed restroom break. That took almost an hour and when we got back onto the freeway we again found ourselves next to the truck with the dog. We apparently didn't lose our place in line.

We had plenty of fuel for the car. We had plenty of water. We had each other.

And the cats. And Frau.

And Frau was a trooper. We enjoyed our visit to Dallas and I don't recall Frau ever being in a better mood. Frau loved to travel, I guess, even at only a few miles an hour.

On Frau and our Israel Trip

Darling and I dreamed of visiting Israel and the opportunity arose in 2006 when our church arranged a group tour.

Such a trip necessitated a number of discussions about Darling's mother. After all, the trip lasted eleven days, including travel time. It just wasn't possible that Frau could manage without help for that many days. Or that the house would survive our absence.

Frau decided she would simply return to her home in downtown Houston and stay there while we were gone. After all, she'd only been absent for five years and the summer temperatures rarely reached over a hundred degrees. Indoors. In the shade. With a fan blowing. How hard could that be?

Darling and I agreed that her Mom would perish in the old house. We didn't even discuss the questionable neighbors in the run-down halfway house that was next door to her old home. After all, that was there before and the residents all adored the old woman. In fact, the men in the halfway house took care of her yard for her without Frau asking. This might be because Frau refused to sign the petition to remove the halfway house from the neighborhood. They probably also welcomed the occasional meals and snacks she brought them.

Darling's amazing youngest brother said Frau could stay with him while we were gone, and it was settled. Frau had a wonderful time at her son's house and spoke of it often in later years. We were off to Israel with our church group!

Excited about our upcoming trip, Frau called her sister, Elle, in Germany. "Darling and Darling's husband are going to Israel. Yes, yes, they are going to Israel. They will stop in to see you!" (Frau didn't say "Darling" but used her daughter's name. She did refer to me as simply her husband. Just clarifying that.)

I rolled my eyes and thought about finding a world map. In my mind's eye I could see the entire discussion.

"Look," I'd say, pointing at the country of Israel on the map as Frau sat enraptured in front of me. "This is where we are going." With a flourish I'd move my pointing finger and center it on Frankfurt. "This is not where we are going." I'd smile politely. "It's a long distance apart. We can't just pop over for lunch and see Tanta Elle."

Frau would clap her chubby little hands and beam at me. "Oh, you're so smart! I see it all now. Thank you for making it all so clear."

I'd walk away, triumphant in my mastery of debate.

Of course, none of that happened except in my mind. Within a week Darling informed me that she arranged our return tickets for a three day stay in Frankfurt so we could spend some time with her distant German cousins.

The trip to Israel can be summed up in just a short sentence: we ran where Jesus walked. What an amazing country with a deep history and culture! At the end of the eleven days both of us sat on the return plane, sunburned and exhausted.

Darling's German relatives didn't even know what Darling looked like. Her sweet cousins, Ursel and Werner, met us at the Frankfurt airport, prominently displaying a cardboard sign with Darling's name penciled on it.

So we did spend three wonderful days in Oberkirche, Germany. Ursel and Werner fed us and let us sleep, then took us on a tour of a local castle and gardens. We also had a nice luncheon outside with Frau's sister, Darling's Tanta Elle and Elle's children and grandchildren. Looking lean and fit, Tanta Elle sat quietly then spoke up, speaking

German. "This is my sister from America!" She pointed at Darling. When corrected that Darling was her niece, she nodded and smiled. After a short pause, her eyes brightened and she'd point at Darling. "Who are you and how many children do you have?" she asked in German. This short conversation was repeated a number of times.

At one point Tanta Elle said she missed speaking Polish. Tired as I was, I burst into the chorus from Bobby Vinton's "My Melody of Love" or at least as much of it as I remembered (which, according to Google, is "Moja droga jacie kocham means that I love you so"). When I finished, blushing as I realized I actually sang, Tanta Elle looked at me suspiciously. "That wasn't Polish," she said in German. Thanks, Bobby Vinton.

That trip to Germany was a delightful time and remains a precious memory to me. It never would have happened if Frau hadn't told her sister we'd drop by. Or if I had a globe in the house.

On Frau and Doctors

Doctors. Frau and I agree on this one. We like them just fine, but we don't think they are infallible. I guess we figure they are just like other people, except they wear white coats most of the day and get a lot more people visiting them. They also make a good living from our paychecks. Frau often told Darling "They are milking me like a cow." I never responded to that line.

I like my doctor and I like his assistants. They are all very friendly. When I show up they always ask how I'm doing. I'm never sure how to answer that; I'm there because I'm sick, after all. But I tell them I'm mostly okay, and they nod sympathetically, apparently privy to information that St. Peter has my name on a short list.

Then they ask me how Frau is doing.

Well, truthfully, that's because Darling is with me, isn't it? Everyone loves Darling and she's a regular at the Doctor's office, dispensing hugs to all the medical personnel within reach. She always goes with me. I can drive myself, which Frau cannot, but I think she's afraid I would just hop over to the local diner and wait an hour and come home. Perhaps with some justification.

So they are really asking Darling how Frau is doing. All the nurses love Frau. They think she is adorable. I keep telling them they are free to take Frau home and adopt her, which earns me a pathetic smile from some of them and a deserved eye-roll from Darling, who puts up with a lot worse than that from me.

Frau visits the Doctor pretty often. All the doctors in our clinic know her. And, to be fair, she is charming and adorable with them all. She loves people, after all, and people can tell. Most of the visits follow a familiar pattern, repeated like a solemn litany. The Doctor (or Nurse) asks Frau how she is, to which Frau responds cheerfully that she is "fine." Darling then sighs and explains all the latest symptoms.

This time Frau goes to the Doctor, explaining that she doesn't feel so well and they determine that she has low oxygen in her blood. Up until that point I guess I didn't even know they measured that sort of thing. I mean, if it's blue, that's bad. If it's red, that's good, unless you are seeing a lot of it.

Well, of course, Frau has some trouble breathing, doesn't she? The walk from the bedroom suite to the kitchen exhausts her. And she doesn't even swim in the pool any more, which is too bad, because it made me smile when I'd hear her paddle around in the evening singing to herself. At least somebody was having a good time in all that water.

Our Doctor is a great guy, and I wouldn't mind going golfing with him or something, but I only see him when I'm sick. Besides, he tells me he doesn't golf - he runs marathons. He listens to Frau's heart and lungs, then checks her other vitals. He slaps a prescription on Frau for oxygen.

Two contraptions were delivered to the house. One is a big box, about half again as tall as one of those mini-fridges that you send to your college kid or smuggle under your desk at work. There's a long, clear tube connected to it. "Don't run this out more than fifty feet," says the guy. "And I set all the settings per the instructions from the doctor. Don't light any matches near the machine." That was my first plan, of course.

The other contraption is an oxygen bottle with a little stand. Frau is required to take the clear tube and connect it to that bottle whenever she goes somewhere outside of the house.

I don't remember how many weeks that went on. She'd amble out of her suite with this plastic tubing trailing behind her. "My leash," she called it. "I feel like a pet dog," she said. We had to move the machine to the back of her closet so the noise wouldn't become too bothersome for her, or for us, for that matter.

My Mother-in-law Misadventures

I'm not sure what that box did, but it was supposed to be concentrating the oxygen in the air and pumping the high-grade stuff through the tube. Hence the no-match rule. You don't want flames near concentrated oxygen.

Frau loves to go places, and Darling obliges most of the time. Now Frau had to take the oxygen bottle with her, the thin tubes feeding her oxygen. She didn't want to go anywhere because of the oxygen bottle and the "leash" that had to go with her.

Besides the machine, Frau had to endure a therapist coming over and checking her breathing, explaining how badly she needed to stay connected to the concentrated air. Just to add insult to injury, the machine and bottle were rentals, so there were fees to pay. Frau muttered about those costs for weeks.

I'm not sure what the final straw was, but one day she had Darling call the delivery guy to come pick the equipment up. As far as she was concerned she was finished with that treatment. She doesn't seem to be breathing any better, but she doesn't seem to be breathing worse either.

At least we can light candles in the house again.

On Frau and People

"How old do you think I am?"

That was Frau's favorite question of people in social situations. By social situations, I mean any time that someone stopped and spoke to Frau.

She genuinely loved people and that delight in others showed. All the nurses at the Doctor's office adored her, as I previously mentioned. It amazed me how easily others took a liking to the old lady.

One time during the early years together, when she was still capable of walking (although slowly) I took her with me to a local book store. I'm a guy and I don't like shopping, but I knew what I was after and for some odd reason I invited her to come along. Maybe it was because she sat in the living room watching me with sad puppy dog eyes as I got ready to leave.

She took my arm as we slowly shuffled into the store. I wasn't entirely sure where she wanted to go, but I've been going to bookstores for decades and almost all of them have spots for people to sit and read, so I wasn't worried. Well, I was a little worried. I didn't need to be.

The first thing we spotted upon entering the store was a group of tables off to the right that were associated with the attached coffee shop.

"I'll sit there," she said, pointing to one of the tables.

"There's a guy at that table," I whispered. I don't know why I whispered. We were in a book store, not a library. She didn't reply and we headed toward the group of tables, a number of which were entirely vacant of occupants.

"Hello," she smiled at the young man seated at the table. He was drinking coffee and reading a book. "Do you mind if I sit here?" Frau said as she sat down across from him.

His return smile was equally bright. "Please do," he responded.

I just shrugged and smiled at him. "Do you want some coffee?" I asked Frau. She asked for a glass of water and I got that for her.

I headed off to my book section searching for the book I wanted. Finding my book took me longer than I expected. Finding my book always takes me longer than I expect. Perhaps it's genetic. My youngest daughter has exactly the same problem.

When I returned with my book (and another excellent choice) I checked out at the counter. Frau was still sitting at the table and she and the young man were engaged in a lively discussion. I felt badly about interrupting them.

"Well," she said as she struggled to her feet, "it is time to go." She beamed at the young man and he smiled back as he returned to his book. "It was so nice to meet you and God bless you."

"Thank you, ma'am. It was nice meeting you, too." He watched her as we left.

"What a nice young man," she said as she settled into the car. "He thought I was only fifty years old." She laughed about that and proceeded to tell me everything she learned about him in the half hour they had together. I don't remember anything she told me about the young man, but I do remember the sparkle he put into an old woman's eyes. Wherever he is, bless his heart.

I'm sure that she prayed for him in her prayers that night. I'm equally sure she smiled when she thought of looking so young.

On Frau and Cable TV, again

I don't know what to say. I thought I fixed the remote so Frau cannot possibly mess up her television cable, and she really didn't - well, I don't think she did. But last night Darling called me into Frau's room to check the television. Frau's room is wall-to-wall STUFF and she lives in the margins of a footpath between her chair, her bed and the bathroom.

She does have a nice television.

I probably mentioned it is a large flat-screen. Every time I touch it (maybe three times now) I quiver. It's just that nice. Computer inputs in the back, cable connections, A/V connections. I think of all the games I could play while watching this television and my fingers twitch.

Anyway, cable seemed to be okay, but the picture was black and white. It didn't matter which cable station; all I got was a black and white picture. I couldn't get it to change. So I dug past some chairs and boxes and footstools and more boxes and maybe a pillow or two and got to the power plug and unplugged it. That's the correct technical response to hardware failure. (Except for the furniture rearrangement.) I waited and plugged the television back in.

Black and white.

Nice black and white. Don't get me wrong. The picture was great, but there wasn't a tinge of color in the entire screen. Shades of grey.

She has the remote, I thought. And she does. It's behind the television, though I shudder when I think of her using it. I guarantee we'd be back to the days of Darling having to reset the cable channel at least once a day, sometimes more.

I study the remote. Buttons for changing the screen settings including the one to make it go full-screen, which she insists on, though I think everyone looks short and wide. Maybe it's just me. (Take that both ways - it was meant as a double entendre.) There are settings for viewing in computer mode and picture-in-picture and sleep mode. I looked for the Escape key hoping it would get me out of there, but it didn't have one.

My Mother-in-law Misadventures

So the TV remote wasn't my answer.

I carefully study the Cable remote. Nothing helps me. I am stumped. A small bubble bursts in my joy over the television, thinking it is broken and needs to be repaired. My cynical side knew it was just too good to last.

Then it occurs to me. Somehow she managed to change the channel. Not to a channel that doesn't get the cable signal. No, that would be too easy. To a channel that only gets the signal in black and white. I don't know how she does it, but I changed to the correct TV channel and we're back to a Technicolor picture, crisp and sparkling. Western guns are blazing.

I'm telling you, my computer would look great on that television.

On Frau and Eye Surgery

When Frau came to live with us she wore thick glasses and used a large magnifying glass to read. A few years after living with us, Darling took her to an eye doctor, who diagnosed Frau with cataracts and recommended surgery to correct them. As far as I could tell, this was outpatient surgery and had no impact on my life at all.

That's the way I like it.

The day before the surgery Frau actually smiled at me as she wandered back into her room. "Tomorrow," she said, "I won't need glasses any more to read."

I had my doubts, but I didn't know anything about cataract surgery. Maybe it was possible. I did not dash her hopes, but I turned to Darling. "Will she be able to see well enough to get rid of the glasses entirely?" I asked, both my eyebrows rising.

"We'll find out," said Darling.

I was home before they returned from the Doctor. Apparently with this surgery they fix your eyes and send you home, the cure complete and no further work needed.

Darling and Frau walked in, Frau slowly of course. She had her eyes fixed, not her legs. Frau was not wearing glasses and she headed off to her room.

Darling and I talked a bit in the kitchen, getting dinner ready. Darling assured me the surgery went well.

Suddenly there was an ear-splitting scream from Frau's room and Darling ran in there. I wondered what heavy weapon I could use to defeat the monster that occupied the room while it was vacant. Whatever critters invaded were undoubtedly after the snack foods hidden away in there.

Darling returned with tears in her eyes. At my questioning look she started laughing again. "It's okay," she patted my arm. "Mom looked in the mirror and was shocked. 'Oh, my!' she said. 'I am ten years older! Look! My face has wrinkles.'"

Darling reassured her mother that she looked the same as usual. I guess that eye surgery worked after all.

On Willow Trees and Weeping

So let's talk about the willow tree.

My Mom loved willow trees. She told me that the giant willow outside my aunt's house was planted by her when she was a child. Her Grandma sent her out for a willow switch once when she misbehaved. After getting switched Mom said she planted that twig in the side yard. Apparently it thrived, since the willow that I remember was a towering giant, leafy branches swaying against the blue sky.

I never did ask which tree she got the switch from though. You just didn't ask those kinds of questions or you'd be looking for a switch of your own.

So I have a fondness for willow trees myself. We had one in the back yard of the house I grew up in. Yes, they are messy. So what? They stay outdoors. It isn't like they come tramping mud and leaves into the house. My brothers and I had that job, and we were quite good at it.

So I commiserate with Frau about the willow tree.

She has a fondness for willow trees for a very different reason. When the Nazi soldiers took residence in her house (and made her "a servant in her own home") they were mean men and young Hertha was an easy target for their bad intentions.

For some reason, an infraction of the rules or just plain meanness, the soldiers got angry at her and her husband at different times. During one of these episodes, in the evening, they were seeking for Frau, a young woman alone against armed and angry men. She had nowhere to hide, so she huddled down by the trunk of the willow tree in their back yard, praying for help. The guards walked within a few feet of her under that willow tree and never saw her. That's not the only time the soldiers hunted her, but it is the only time that I know where the willow tree saved her.

So she cried when we bought the house, since it had a willow tree in the backyard. And, as she says, it is the only willow she ever knew that actually weeps on you as you stand under it. That's true. I was surprised when I stood under the tree and felt the small drops on my arms. Houston humidity and all that. I don't know. Maybe that willow was just sad.

The point is that she was fond of that willow.

It's a pretty big tree, a good fifty feet into the air, maybe a bit more. There used to be two main trunks, one leaning into our yard and one leaning out of it, over the fence. The inner trunk died and we took that down years ago. Of course I liked the tree even more then. Now I'm getting some shade, and it's dropping its wee limbs and leaves into the neighbor's yard instead of mine.

But a few weeks ago the neighbor mentioned to my wife that the tree had to come down, since it was breaking the fence. I went out and looked, and he was right. The trunk, a good two feet in diameter, was leaning pretty heavily on the top of the fence between us, and the fence was surely going to lose that battle.

So I talked to the neighbor and mentioned I'd cut some of the branches right away, but we needed to get a tree specialist to drop the main limbs, since they had to be dropped between the fence and his garage. I got permission to go into his yard and get the branches out. I was hoping he'd say no, that he didn't want me back there and he'd take care of it. No such luck.

That Saturday I took my little bow saw, designed to cut limbs with impunity, and examined the tree. I was cutting trees down and helping my Dad create cords of firewood when I was ten years old. I'm not Paul Bunyan, but I'm not Pee-Wee Herman either. After some consideration I figured I could take the limbs down without endangering his property. (You're expecting me to say I crushed his garage or the fence or both. I didn't.)

Now trust me when I say this; I'm not a big fan of heavy labor. It's hot outside and I'm not good with heat. And I'm not as young as I used to be (I was never as young as I used to be). So I cut one of the main branches (there were three), and it fell in my neighbor's back yard. I went and tossed the pieces into our yard. Then I cut the second main branch, rested and tossed those pieces back into my yard and rested. Then I cut part of the final branch and rested. I finished cutting it and rested some more. Then I cut some pieces and tossed them into our yard. And rested. And threw a twig over the fence. And rested. Cutting that last branch almost did me in, and Darling helped me drag it around the yard and drop it just outside our fence, where it rested for a week, until I could get my growing giant of a son to haul it into the back yard (bless his heart).

Darling said I was beet red and needed to get into the pool. So I handed her my belt and walked into the water wearing all my clothes. That's the benefit of a personal pool. Nobody tells me what to wear, or not wear, when I go swimming.

I might point out that each of the cut branches fell almost perfectly, and there was no damage to fence or garage – and great benefit to my ego.

We finished cutting the willow down the next weekend. We borrowed a chainsaw from my neighbor to cut through the base of the trunk. The saw blade wasn't sharp, and it took a while, with me, Darling and the Lad taking turns at running the saw. Then my good-hearted son bagged the branches. (Bless his heart again.)

Frau came out and watched us take the tree down the final few cuts. She saw we had the axe out and for some reason wanted to take a swing at the tree. I was all for it; everybody should get into the fun if they want. But Darling wouldn't let her, and with good reason, probably. I guess we want to avoid a trip to the emergency room if possible.

Frau was upset we had to cut the willow down. Really, I don't blame her. I miss it, though I still have some fairly good-sized branches to clean up. There's something about a weeping willow that we both like. Now the willow is gone, and all that remains is the weeping, in some part of Frau and some part of me.

On Frau and Yoda

The beginning of Frau's love affair with Yoda comes to me secondhand, mostly from the Lass. As she told me, Frau was walking to the kitchen for coffee when she noticed Yoda on television; the Lass and the Lad were watching Star Wars™ (probably the one with Luke finally getting some Jedi training). She stopped on the way to the kitchen and exclaimed to the children "Who is that, the little man?" Then she laughed. "Why, he is as old and wrinkled as I am!"

Thinking back on Yoda in the second movie, I think I agree with that assessment. When Frau got her coffee she stopped in the living room and watched Yoda for a while. Without a doubt, she was smitten.

Whenever she brought him up in conversation she smiled and a dreamy look floated across her face. ("What is his name, again? The little man, who is old like me?") She couldn't remember his name, but she couldn't forget him either.

This lasted for years. As a Star Wars™ fan, the movie was on my television more often than most, so she could at least indulge her fantasy on occasion. ("What is his name again? The little man?")

Her affection for Yoda made me smile. I do recall once while I was watching The Revenge of the Sith, I paused the television as she came through the room. "Really," I said, "you want to see this. Yoda kicks some serious butt in this one." She sat and watched her hero make awesome acrobatic Jedi moves against his Sith opponent. The Force was strong within him. At least she didn't notice Yoda was younger in that one.

Her infatuation with the small green Jedi Master gave me the opportunity for a number of Perfect Presents. One year I bought her a small bobble-head version of Yoda, which took up residence in a place in her room where she could see him all the time. Another year, for her birthday, I found the ideal item - a Yoda backpack. If you didn't know it was a backpack, it was perfectly suited as an almost-life-size version of the alien teacher.

Frau's birthday party went pretty well. Grandchildren and children came and wished her happy birthday with presents and snacks. I made her a cheesecake, the kind that you cook. The cheesecakes I make are very dense; this one probably weighed five pounds. We saved her Yoda present for last. When she unwrapped Yoda she started to laugh, a long low deep belly laugh that shook her from her toes to her pinned-up grey hair. She sat at the table with her new Yoda and laughed and slapped the table with her right palm. We had cheesecake and she took a bite. Then she looked at her new pal Yoda and laughed more. This went on for over an hour. I was a little afraid she might not be able to get a breath.

That Yoda got a special place next to her chair in her room. I'm just glad she didn't get posters and put them up on the walls. Rock star Yoda - just what every room needs.

One evening she came from the kitchen heading toward her room. "Oh, look! It is Yoda!" she said, as I watched the television. This time she remembered the name of our favorite Jedi Master, but I was frightened a little.

"No, no, no." I said firmly. "That is Gollum, and he is not a nice guy like Yoda." Frau's face fell when she realized she was looking at an imposter.

When I watch Star Wars™ movies now, Yoda seems sadder than I remember. Perhaps he knows his fan club is a trifle smaller.

On Frau and Banks

One of the things that bothers me about Frau is that she spends much of her time sitting in her room poring over her financial statements. Like Scrooge McDuck, but less active and without the cravat. I think she harbors some strange thought that it isn't real if she doesn't count it. She is constantly angry at one bank or another, often accusing them of stealing her money. Now I'm not talking about a hundred dollars here. If it were that little I'd write her a check just to get her to be quiet about it.

Two notable instances come to mind. A few years ago she was convinced that the bank had lost a certain number of thousand dollars. They actually stole it, she said. These misplaced funds were the topic of conversation from her for every meal we had, and the opening line of every salutation when she came out of her room. I didn't get involved, but I think the upshot was that she took some of the money and put it in another account, losing track of doing so. The bank also lost track of it, a fact which astounds and frightens me. It took a long visit to the bank and Darling's youngest brother to resolve that one. The moral of that is sometimes the banks do make mistakes, so keep close watch on your money!

Another situation occurred more recently, the same sort of thing. This time the bank stole a certain thousand dollars of her money, and she could prove it. She had read and studied all her statements and one month the money was there, the next it was gone. Thieves! Another long session at the bank did not resolve the problem, and she was working into such a snit that she wanted all her money in cash. She was going to simply keep it in her room. We're talking quite a few dollars here. This theft dominated conversations, to the point where she wasn't sleeping and she would wander through the house at all hours distraught by the calumny of the banking institutions. I had enough and got Darling to get a listing of all bank transactions in the last two years. Everything balanced, but there was one month where that amount of money was phone transferred, and the recipient was not specified. I circled that, gave it to her and told her to get the bank to provide specifics. That took me ten minutes, twenty tops. I don't know how it turned out, and maybe it isn't over yet, but I don't hear any more of it, and that's the point.

I think basically Frau hates banks. It's just a principle of hers and nothing personal. Looking back on her life we can see that she and Adolf lost a lot of money that was left in the banks in Poland. Some letters in the early sixties showed they tried to obtain the missing funds but it seems they were not successful, or perhaps only moderately reimbursed. The war destroyed her trust in banks and the banks didn't work very hard to restore that trust.

She gets along fine with the people in the banks, but people love her and she loves them and even bank people can tell that. In the time I have known her, Frau has moved her money into no less than four banks, and maybe more. The last bank manager was quite saddened when she closed her accounts, though I cannot really get my head around that. Frau is just too high maintenance from my perspective. Really, is all that grief worth a few percent? What she probably needs is a money manager, but I might as well stick her with a pin as suggest that. I tried it once and she told me the story of investing her money in the stock market with some relatives and how she lost it all.

She did ask me once what she should do with her money. I was shocked. After a few moments of thinking about it I suggested she give it all away. Buy some wells for people in Africa and India. Start a few churches in other countries. Spend it well, but let it all go. You would have thought I shot her in the head. I don't believe I have ever seen such a fast exit from a room.

It isn't that she needs the money. She has no bills and is fed with a roof over her head. Frau made one dinner in all our years in this house, and that was pork chops and dumplings. I was appreciative, though I am not a big pork chop fan and cleanup was a chore, but that's okay. I've never once seen her do a load of laundry, mop, vacuum or dust. I mean, I'd love to have a life where I don't need to do any of those things.

Wait. I have a life like that. Darling does all those things for both of us.

I think I'll blame the banks.

On Darling and DC

Darling wanted to go with some friends to DC for a pro-life rally and to tour some of the capitol sights. She's never been and these friends are the right mixture for her to go with. The pickle, of course, is that she will not go unless someone can care for her Mom.

Now Frau and I agree on this point: Nobody needs to take care of her, at least most of the time. But Darling won't go on her trip if someone responsible isn't looking out for her Mom.

We discussed Frau going to stay with her eldest son. The eldest was concerned that his Mom wouldn't be comfortable at his house. He pointed out they have dogs and cats and birds and their house is a mess and ... the list of issues was staggering and I was pretty disappointed. It's not like Frau needs to go jogging in the house. She pretty much finds a spot to sit and stays there. It's the moving from spot to spot that's hard for her. I guess that's what the eldest son is concerned about, the lack of room to maneuver.

His wife volunteers to stay at our house while Darling is gone. Frau isn't for that at all! Once again we agree. I'm staying at the house during this week, so I certainly get a vote.

At this point Darling is not planning to go with her friends on this road trip. She just doesn't think Frau can be alone that much. Nonsense, says I. She's alone that much all week by choice. She won't go hungry - she can get to the kitchen and we have no idea what snack-type foods are hidden away in her room. Darling still isn't comfortable with the idea. Darling's friends push her some; they really want her to go with them.

Out of the blue another dear friend calls and says she will take the week off work and stay with Frau during the day. Darling makes plans to go on the trip. She makes some of her awesome chili and puts it in the freezer. I'm delighted with that part.

I talk it over with her. How about if her friends call and check on Frau? Less impact all around. She won't go hungry, I promise.

Another friend volunteers to check on Frau while Darling is out of town. So plans are made, bags are packed and Darling is off on a road trip to DC with her friends for a week, leaving at three in the morning on Saturday.

The kids and I play computer games and such on Saturday. I offer lunch to Frau, but she turns me down, making a trip or two to the kitchen on her own. I buy a chicken and we have chicken and potatoes for dinner. Church the next day, and the kids and I go for TexMex. We bring leftover fajitas home to Frau, but she has already dined on - what are those fish? Sardines? Herring? AUGH! For dinner I order pizza. I'm quite the cook.

The kids have Monday off from school, so I stay home and we have another day together. We watch a few movies and eat leftovers. Frau has some as well. The Lad starts feeling badly.

The next day he is sick, so I am off to work for the morning and home in time to feed him lunch. I feed him leftovers, mostly the fajitas. I was obviously betting the food wasn't the culprit. I finish the pizza. I invite Frau to have some, but she is content with her fish, she says. Our eldest daughter drops by to check on her Grandmother and spends some time. That's nice. I heat frozen chili that night for dinner.

So now we're on Wednesday of the week, the two youngest are off at their mother's house, and I need to make up some hours at work. I talk with Darling and ask her to tell Frau to manage on her own for dinner. When I get home I am almost straight to bed. I am not sleeping well with Darling gone. I have cleaned a few drawers and cupboards. Darling has a mild panic attack about that when I tell her.

Thursday I put four or five garbage bags out on the curb for the garbage man. When I get home the Lad and I have chili and I give some to Frau. The Lass is at a friend's house making cookies for an international festival at school on Friday. She has leftovers when she gets home.

We lost the cat, the little one, the one that plays fetch. I realize I haven't seen him in a while.

It's true the cat was mad at me when Darling left and made himself scarce, but he still appeared briefly in the shadows. Now he is nowhere to be found. The kids and I search for him, but no luck. I open every room upstairs and every closet. I open the garage and call for him. Nothing. I don't think he escaped outside, but I can't think of another scenario.

Friday morning is hectic and I take the Lad to school, which makes me a little late. I make it up at the end of the day. On the way home I pick up some chicken sandwiches and give one to Frau. The Lass drops by to pick something up for the Lad and I have her go into Frau's room and check for the missing cat. He is still missing. Frau hasn't seen him either.

Saturday morning I leave early and work until about noon. I get home and clean, thoroughly. The house needs it. I do a few loads of laundry. Make the bed. Look for the cat. Run the vacuum. Look for the cat. Mop the floor. Look for the cat. Clean the bathrooms. Look for the cat.

Darling gets home at nine in the evening and hears something. She opens the garage door and the little cat appears. So I didn't lose the cat. He would just rather spend the days in the garage, cold and hungry and in the dark than spend those days in the house with me while Darling is gone.

Ouch.

But at least I didn't lose him. And Frau weathered Darling's trip just fine.

On Frau and Head Injuries

This is the sort of thing that Darling is afraid of. I finally get it.

Sunday morning, we're all a bit hurried, but not too badly, getting around and eating breakfast. Frau's door creaks. Frau stands in the doorway. I say good morning, though I am never sure if she hears me or not. She asks where Darling is.

"Upstairs. Getting ready for church."

"I need her. I have to show her something."

I hear the blow drier stop in the upstairs bathroom and I yell up the stairs to Darling that her mother needs her. She comes down and they disappear into Frau's room for a while. Darling calls to me that she needs some ointments from upstairs, which I get for her.

Later Darling comes out, a bit tuckered. Frau hit her head. Apparently she was sitting on the edge of her tub and lost her balance and fell in. She cut the back of her head. There was quite a bit of blood. Darling is stressed.

We come home from church and Frau comes out for lunch, the back of her head matted with blood, the bandage hanging precariously by the tape on her hair. The wound has been bleeding again. Darling puts another bandage on it, with a hair band to hold it in place. Frau probably needed some stitches, but she isn't going to the Doctor. "It's only a cut," she says, "and they milk me like a cow for my money."

So I get it. I see what makes Darling nervous about leaving Frau alone. Or even alone with me.

On Frau and the Painted Churches

I wanted my wedding anniversary with Darling to be special. She was tired of caring for her mother for so many years, and I thought it was time for an outing. It took me very little time to talk her into a day's drive to get away from the house. She called her sister in law who sweetly promised to drop by and check on Frau. We packed some snacks, grabbed a camera and headed west.

I don't love to drive, usually. I'm easily frustrated by all the other people on the roads. Give me an open road, though, and I'm okay. The highway going west from Houston to San Antonio opens up and runs straight into tomorrow, to where adventures await.

I actually did some research before we took this little day trip. I printed a map of special churches around a small city called Schulenburg, right off from Interstate-10. We spent a few hours driving and I turned off on some smaller roads.

"Where are we going?" Darling was probably astounded that I planned ahead.

"I have a map of some churches." I was very proud.

"Churches?" Darling sounded doubtful.

"Painted churches," I added, quite pleased with myself. I handed her the folded map. "See? They're marked on this map."

Normally when I tell a travel tale it is fraught with missed turns, lost patience, and GPS devices full of mendacity. The tales end badly. For everyone. Never, ever expect to get anywhere on time if I say the dreaded words "Hey! I know a shortcut."

Over the years Darling endured a number of these incidents first-hand, so I understood why she was concerned. Yet, in spite of my personal driving acumen, we followed the map and went successfully from one Painted Church to another.

I don't know how best to describe the Painted Churches. When German and Czech immigrants came to Texas in the late 1800s and early 1900s they left great cathedrals behind in their native countries. The immigrants, of course, were not wealthy and could only afford to build the small wooden or stone churches that we pass almost anywhere in the southern states. The interiors of the painted churches, however, are resplendent with painted murals, vaulting arches and stained glass windows. Walking through the unassuming front doors of the churches, we stepped into the heavenly realms often viewed in the cathedrals of Europe.

Each church was unique, both on the outside and also on the inside. In some we encountered others visiting, but usually the churches sat empty except for the spiritual peace that dwelt within. In the last church we visited we met a small family. They were praying for a miracle healing for their daughter who had cancer and a resolution for their financial difficulties. Darling spoke quietly with them for a while and then prayed with them, tears in her eyes.

We stopped for dinner and went home. I think the trip helped give Darling a much-needed break from the daily care-taking and, perhaps, refreshed her spirit. I had a great time.

The next day, of course, Darling's mother asked about our trip and Darling showed her the pictures, in full color on our computer.

"Oh, my, that is gorgeous," Frau said, and she clapped her hands, slowly in approval of the workmanship and beauty. At one point she said "How I would like to see these Painted Churches!"

My Mother-in-law Misadventures

Darling looked at me and we planned another adventure for a few weeks into the spring, when the wildflowers would be blooming.

Springtime in Texas can be beautiful. I'm sure it's beautiful in a lot of other areas too, but it's the wildflowers in Texas that always make me happy when the cool breeze of spring whispers against my skin here in Houston. The bluebonnets and Indian paintbrushes garnish the landscape as you go west toward San Antonio, just as you get into the Hill Country. The area around the Painted Churches is bedecked with wildflowers in the spring.

A few weeks later I was driving west again with Darling and this time we had Frau with us.

We saw the churches a second time and the spring flowers blossomed in great abundance, perhaps welcoming Frau to the verdant landscape of west Texas. If anything, we had a better time than the previous trip, though it was hard for Frau to walk from the car to some of the smaller churches. These churches are old and not designed for easy access.

Frau walked in each church and sighed a great, deep sigh of contentment. In each one she slowly ambled to a pew and knelt, bowing her head in prayer, her small chubby hands clasped tightly together. She spent long minutes talking to the Almighty and I'm sure He spoke back to her. She glowed with the reflected beauty of the church interiors.

Often during the trip she had me pull over to the side of the country roads, sometimes getting out and sometimes simply staring through her open car window at the beautiful panorama of wildflowers stretching across the fields. We stopped at the same restaurant in Schulenburg that we stopped at previously. Frau had pork chops and dumplings. I think it was the end of a nearly perfect day for her.

Darling and Frau were both happy. And I didn't even get lost.

On Frau and Taxes

Tax time rolls around every year. I'm not too happy with it, especially when I estimated wrong and we have to pay, like this year. I don't know anybody who likes taxes, except our accountant.

Our tax man came over to the house to get our paperwork. He's a nice guy. This is the only time of year that we see him, which is too bad. He probably has more free time in other months of the year. I asked how he was doing and he grinned. "Just finished telling a guy he owed $680,000 in taxes." Ouch, I say. "Oh, don't feel too bad for him. He made over two million, so he has the money." As he takes our paperwork Darling tells him he needs to talk to Frau.

"Love to," he says, and he means it. Frau comes limping out of her room and doesn't even smile at him. He grins at her. "You ready for me to do your taxes? Have your paperwork together?" I'm telling you, our tax guy is just an amiable bundle of joy.

Frau frowns at him. "I'm not going to pay taxes this year."

"You have to pay taxes or they put you in a little room with bars and no windows." He says that and I'm thinking that's pretty close to what Frau deals with now, by choice. The current room is nicer and she has a window, though. Either way someone would deliver her food, I suppose.

"When you're my age you shouldn't have to pay taxes. I read that after you are eighty you don't need to pay taxes anymore." Frau's lower lip trembled as she said these words.

Our tax guy, once again, takes it in stride. "It wasn't true last year, and it isn't true this year. You always have to pay taxes."

"Maybe she's thinking of another country" I chime in. Darling and our tax guy look at me like I've lost my mind and I decide it's best to just be silent. Frau doesn't even look at me, but that's because I spoke at a normal volume and she didn't hear me. I'm thinking I need to go clean the pool.

"I gave money to my children and grandchildren this year. I'm not going to pay taxes."

Then a short discussion ensues concerning this particular issue. Giving away money to relatives does not help with your taxes, and has no impact on what you pay. It might impact the recipients, but not at the amount she gave everyone. I remain silent and leave for my upstairs chair. I can still hear everything.

"Well, I'm not paying. I shouldn't have to pay taxes any more. I'm an old lady and I have paid enough to the government." From her point of view, I can easily agree. I am sure she has paid a lot of money to the government and at her age it amounts to a considerable sum. But you have to wince a bit when someone says they paid enough to the government? By the government reckoning, when is it enough? I'd say when you get buried, but then they get that little bit more in estate taxes, don't they? (And do you notice how I use "they" to mean the government? I can't recall a time when I thought of the government as "of the people, by the people and for the people" and that makes me sad.)

The tax man smiles. "And you have to pay a little more. But your taxes this year are easy, aren't they? Nothing special. You just have to pay tax on your bank income. You should have received those statements in the mail. Gather them up and I'll do your taxes for you."

Some small chit-chat later, with our tax man telling one of his jokes and he's gone, off to compute our taxes.

Frau retreats to her room, possibly to do battle with her paperwork. Eventually I send my check in to the IRS and go back to work so I can send them more next year. The tax guy does her taxes and Frau sends her check and disappears to pout in her room for some number of days, probably related to the dollar amount. She eats in her room and I don't see her until she is no longer angry about taxes. The tax debacle lasts a few weeks and then it's over.

For this year.

On Frau and Microwaves

You could call it an ordeal. Over the past few years Darling worked hard to teach Frau some semblance of cooking independence that minimized the risk of burning the house down. That excluded the stove and oven, and probably excluded the toaster oven, too.

That's why I am thankful for the microwave. God bless the people who invented the microwave oven. I cannot explain in any detail the training required for Frau to learn to use the microwave. At some point she finally grasped the concept. She can make her own meals as long as it involves heating leftovers in the microwave or making instant oatmeal using the microwave.

Breakfast oatmeal is a daily ritual for Frau.

Don't get me wrong. I am proud of her for figuring it all out. That microwave has about twenty buttons too many in my opinion. I suspect I don't know how to use it any better than she does, but at least I can look at my food through the little window above the stove.

And then tragedy strikes. Frau was making her microwave oatmeal on Saturday morning and it didn't cook. The micros no longer waved. Frau was stoic about it all. Since it was Saturday morning I was sitting in the living room with Darling when Frau brought it to our attention.

"My oatmeal didn't cook." We're thinking it's a user problem at that point. So Frau tried again. "It's still cold. That's okay. I can eat it like this."

You would have to hear the tone to appreciate the mastery of that last statement. It made me *want* to get up and cook the oatmeal for her, and that's not easy. Darling got up and checked the microwave. Sure enough, dead as a doornail. She cooked the oatmeal on the stove for her mother.

You don't miss something until it's gone, they say, which certainly seems true when the microwave quits working. We were effectively tethered to the house at mealtimes during the weekend for fear that Frau might starve. Frau used the stove for some soup on Saturday, but when we found the light blue flame happily heating our kitchen ten minutes after she was finished we figured we had best handle it ourselves.

So we are waiting for the microwave repair people. In the meantime, I am watching movies and chomping on kernels of popcorn. Not really. You can buy pre-popped popcorn.

But I sure miss the little things.

On Frau and Computers

Frau was impressed with my new iMac. Shoot, I'm impressed with it. Big screen, bright colors, easy to set up. When I powered it up, the computer asked me which of the many networks I wanted to use and listed them for me. How easy is that? Frau thought the computer was pretty. When I made a video call to my brother up North she was quite impressed that she could see him on the screen. When she discovered that he could see her sitting on the couch next to me, she was downright amazed. I browsed the web to some German web sites and Polish web sites and she read the latest news from countries she hasn't been in for a long time and she seemed really happy.

So I gave her a lesson. I set it up on the kitchen table, gave her the mouse and away we went. Sort of. She didn't really get the mouse concept. Clicking on links seemed strange to her. I guess it is, really. Especially if it's the first time you've seen it. I saw this same problem in one of the classes I taught years ago in a local college. The poor guy just didn't grasp the concept of a mouse moving the cursor. Frau and I played with it for an hour and Frau was really happy and thought about getting a computer.

Her Granddaughter came over and Frau told her how she was going to get an iMac. "No, Grandma, that's not the machine you want. I can get a discount on something else using Windows and you'll like that better." Since it cost less, Frau was all for it.

I have to admit that it surprised me. Granddaughter brought the computer over, and it was a new type of touch screen, so I was actually kind of jazzed, thinking that Frau wouldn't need to worry about that mouse thing. Granddaughter set up the new computer in Frau's room, and I performed a magic ritual to get the Windows™ machine to recognize the wireless internet in the house. So Frau was in her room with Granddaughter for a few hours laughing and giggling, which was pretty nice to hear. And Granddaughter said she had the hang of the mouse and wasn't too keen on the touch the screen part, so she might get a different computer for her, which was too bad, because it looked cool and matched her television. I really like that television.

So Frau was up and running on the Internet. I don't know what sites she was viewing or how much she was doing on it, but she was having a good time. Well, except for the other night when she told Darling that the computer quit working and the television didn't work either. And yes, Frau found and used the television remote control and the television was all messed up and we had to correct that problem (again). The computer was fine, though. It just went to sleep waiting on input and Frau thought it broke.

It is simply a learning curve.

Frau gave up on the computer in less than a week and made Granddaughter take it back. It was just too much. I think the last straw was when she screamed that the computer knew she was sitting at her table and knew her name – and the computer was typing to her! Granddaughter installed an instant messenger and was trying to chat with her Grandma. Frau still appreciated the iMac, but she no longer wanted to own one.

On Hurricane Ike

Humility is not an option, but a requirement.

We speak blithely of "riding out the storm" when a Hurricane approaches. In fact, when the full force of the winds and rain roared over our home the best I could muster was to huddle inside and listen as the storm rode over us. At one point Frau, Darling and I opened the front door, protected by the surrounding brick of the front porch, and felt the impact as bullets of rain bombarded the ground. The storm growled as it ate its way across the neighborhood. Standing there staring from the blackness of our powerless abode into the swirling wind I regretted that we did not leave. Though we do not live in a flood area, the water swirled in our circular street, pushing branches and debris at its whim.

As I started to close the door to escape the assault on our ears, Darling stopped me and held the door open wider. "Do you hear that?" I didn't, for how could my ears detect any distinct sound in that cacophony outside? She called out and our half-feral cat came to the front door where Darling scooped him up and wrapped his wet and dismayed form in a towel. My guess is she heard the cat with her heart. I don't recall that Frau said anything during the onslaught.

Defiance doesn't matter in the face of nature's fury. As the house shuddered around us and I heard the wrenching sound of boards bowing to the winds, boldness and audacity simply vanished. We sat and waited for the eye of the storm to pass over us, none of us able to sleep any longer. The house cats huddled with Darling and Frau on the couch, sometimes nosing their outdoor cousin, who shivered in a warm towel on Darling's lap. We hoped for a few minutes of peace to descend. Instead of the respite of the eye, we were on the edge of the storm and heavy objects continued to defy gravity through the sightless dark of the night.

We knew Ike was approaching, but it was simply a Category 2 Hurricane, so what was the worry? Our newest neighbors moved here from New Orleans after Hurricane Katrina. As we prepared our house for the possible landfall of Ike near us, they evacuated. The Friday night of Ike's arrival we simply watched television to assess the approach of the storm and played on the internet until we lost electricity at about 10pm.

At that point we were simply in a dark and windy night with no power, so we lit some candles, brushed our teeth and went to bed, fairly confident that we would have power restored soon and the storm would simply blow itself out when it hit land.

The rest is history. Ike, like the wolf in the story of the three little pigs, spared some houses and blew others away. Trees were tossed like matchsticks across roads, into ditches, and into the homes of people I know.

We were fortunate. Our house had no damage, though we lost most of our bigger trees. Darling prayed for protection for our house, so I was only mildly surprised that some trees fell one way and others dropped in a different direction. A small pine near the house fell toward the north, some of the branches brushing our back porch. The fir tree fell exactly toward the southwest where it crushed the corner of our shed and stopped short of the fence and the neighbor's garage.

"I should have prayed for God to protect the shed, too," Darling said. I just smiled. It wasn't enough of a dent to worry about.

We had water for the entire time, though all of us in the neighborhood were starved for local information. We survived without electricity for a few days. One neighbor let us run a series of extension cords across the cul-de-sac to power our freezer. After a few days my buddy and I found and purchased a couple generators and got some gas. That took an entire day, and was an adventure all by itself, but we then had a generator for the remainder of a powerless two weeks.

For a few days there were a lot of cookouts as people used the food from their dark freezers and refrigerators before it spoiled. Fences were down everywhere, literally and figuratively.

We met neighbors we didn't know and spent more time with ones we did know. We sat outside in the Houston weather, mercifully cool for a few days after the storm. Others nearby joined us. One neighbor shared ice from the Emergency Response Centers. Another brought us precious gallons of gasoline when we started running low. After clearing fallen debris from our pool, we had a cool place to swim during the days and invited neighbors to take advantage of the cement pond.

Frau took advantage of the pool, often bobbing around with the floats in the clear water, quietly singing songs to herself. Even more than the pool she enjoyed the social time with neighbors, no doubt telling them tales of WWII Poland and Germany.

Before long our curbs were lined with tree limbs and trunks and battered sections of fallen fences. It was a month before the debris in front of our house disappeared and more months before many of my friends had repairs completed on their ravaged homes.

I fixed a couple of bicycles. My children learned to play chess instead of video games. Frau challenged everyone to games of checkers and taught me how to play German checkers, which is an oddly different game. In either version of checkers nobody except Darling could beat her.

"Where did you learn to play checkers like that?" I asked Darling one night after suffering multiple defeats.

She smiled at me. "My Father taught me. Nobody ever beat him." I believed it.

My Mother-in-law Misadventures

Through it all Frau never showed signs of dismay or panic. For fourteen days we had no power except the generator, which we used to keep the freezer and refrigerator running and run a few fans in the house. Frau simply smiled and even seemed delighted at the opportunity to interact with all the neighbors.

The Lass had her seventeenth birthday during this powerless time. We drove to a local restaurant to celebrate, glad to simply sit and eat in the air conditioned interior. Other people had the same idea and the restaurant was packed with people, all smiling and quietly delighted with the trappings of civilization.

We used our generator to power our iMac and played a movie on some of the evenings. My buddy joined us. In the dying daylight our dim living room became our own movie theater, though we lacked the popcorn and sodas. On good days we had ice water. Like many neighbors we shared our ice with those who needed it for coolers.

I don't know if I ever saw Frau as content as she was during the two weeks of recovery from Hurricane Ike in 2008. She showed a constant attitude of acceptance which I hope the children noticed and can emulate. Hers was a strength bred in a person who endured WWII, Nazis, refugee camps and emigration to a new land. It is a strength I can look back at and appreciate.

On Frau and Missing Darling

We headed off this last weekend to take the Lass off to college in Abilene. So we got back from Abilene, eight hours plus to get there Friday night and about the same getting back Sunday. By the time we all get home I'm tired and cranky. Darling and the Lad are tired also and our spirits are low.

Frau comes out of her room less than twenty minutes after we are home. She sits on the little couch and looks at Darling, who is collapsed on her side of the big couch. Now, mind you, Daughter-in-Law took good care of Frau while we were gone. Frau shouldn't have any complaints. Oh, but she does. She sits down and complains how Darling needs to take her to the doctor Monday. The doctor needs to give her fewer pills to take. She says she is taking too many pills and they don't work; they aren't making her better. I'm in the kitchen and I can't take it anymore.

"The doctor can't give you any pills that can fix you," I growl, loud enough that she can hear, which is not subtle. "You're old."

The Lad looks at me like I've lost my mind. Darling doesn't say anything but stares at me as if I transformed into a different person. Frau objects that she isn't old. I could launch into a tirade on how if she'd get up and walk fifty steps a day she'd get a little better, but I just leave the room and go upstairs.

Frau did go to the doctor Monday morning. Monday afternoon she was in the hospital and stayed there until Friday morning. She got a complete blood transfusion because her hemoglobin was too low and they did a myriad of tests looking for the source of the problem, but didn't find anything definitive. She isn't supposed to eat sugars or chocolate or drink coffee. Of course, she was in a drug-induced stupor when the doctor made that proclamation, so she doesn't recall the directions and thinks Darling is lying to her. I figure just give her the coffee and cheesecake and let her munch on the chocolate bars stashed in her room.

I mean, what can they do? They can't make her young again.

Sometimes I just need to shut my mouth and wait until my perspective returns. We have a lot going for us, but sometimes we forget.

On Frau and Mermaids

I liked our pool. I thought I wanted a lap pool so I'd swim and get in better shape, but that's just daydreaming. What I liked most about our pool was that it required very little maintenance.

When we first moved into the big house I wasn't sure how to maintain a pool. I read everything on-line I could find and bought the little kit for testing the water. Diligently I went outside for the next two months, even as the temperature dropped into the forties, and tested the water. I added the chemicals I was supposed to add and carefully followed all the instructions I had. I never let a leaf settle on the bottom, even when I was wearing a wool hat and gloves while I scooped them out.

After a few months I started testing the water once a month. By the time summer rolled around I was just glancing at the pool, smelling the water and cleaning it when I absolutely had to or wanted an excuse to paddle around in a pool and call it working. That was usually sufficient.

When we first moved into the big house I thought the entire family would convene on warm evenings in the pool area and enjoy the benefits of our home-based recreational facility. Sometimes we did, but much less often than I thought.

The person who enjoyed the pool the most was Frau, at least in the early years. The pool was shaped like a kidney, shallow at both ends and deeper in the middle. At each end it came up over my waist and in the middle the water lapped at my chin. Frau, of course, was much shorter than I. She wasn't physically capable of swimming in the pool. Instead she'd get in at the steps with a floaty thing Darling got from the store. She tucked that under her arms and bobbed around the edges of the pool.

Usually Frau went in the pool in the mornings so I wasn't aware of how often she used it. During the longer summer days she sometimes got in the pool in the evenings, when it was partially shaded by the house. On the weekends she sometimes went into the pool while I was busy around the house. I'd see her floating in the pool and impishly press the button that started the waterfall just as she reached the far edge where the water spouted into the pool.

Frau squealed every time, a short scream of delight followed by laughter as she positioned herself to let the water massage her upper back. I laughed every time I did that.

Once in a while during the week I'd come home and I'd sit at the kitchen table and watch her as she floated in the water, quietly singing songs I did not recognize. Perhaps the songs were German or Polish songs she knew as a young girl. I don't know.

I watched her forget her troubles and simply float and sing, the world around her forgotten, the grey hair on the top of her head gently appearing and disappearing at the neared edges of the pool, small wavelets crossing the surface.

That's probably as close to watching a mermaid as I'll ever get. Watching her paddle in the warm pool water, the small waves bouncing from the sides and the sun reflecting in scattered patterns across the surface of the pool simply entranced me. Whatever songs she sang or hummed were the vocal representation of a content life, the siren songs of a person who faced life and managed to still smile, a person who felt the complete relaxation of knowing that life is as simple as swimming in a warm pool in the sunshine.

As the years advanced her trips to the pool lessened and eventually stopped. The siren songs of our own mermaid disappeared entirely.

On Frau and Galveston

Galveston is just a few miles south of us, just over a bridge. You simply drive the width of the island and you're on a Galveston beach. When I lived north of the Mason-Dixon Line, Galveston had the dreamlike quality of palm trees swaying in the salty tang of a sea breeze with blue waters gently lapping against the pristine sand.

Most of the time Galveston is more like the Sahara Desert than a beach, with hot sand underfoot and no shade, though you often get a warm breeze blowing in from the Bay. The waters in the Bay vary from a light muddy brown to a darker brown tinged with seaweed brown. The buoys are painted blue, I think.

Yet we all love to go to Galveston. My Mom had a single item on her to-do list when she visited me years ago: go to Galveston. I took her to Galveston where we spent a delightful time walking on the beach and ambling along the sidewalks of The Strand, which is a fascinating downtown array of stores. Mom bought chocolate fudge. I also took my Mom to Corpus Christi where the blue waters sparkle in the bright sunshine of the southern US coast, but it was Galveston that called to her heart. I get it. Mine, too.

Darling has some good memories of spending summer evenings in Galveston as a child, when Frau took the family to stay in a beach house for a week during summer vacations. Those same memories made Frau smile. Darling also has numerous memories of driving down to the Galveston beaches as a teenager and slowly roasting to a basted-turkey brown, using baby oil as a coating. Kids, don't do that.

When my two youngest were very small I'd pile them into the van early on Saturday mornings and head off to the warm beaches in Galveston. We'd stop at Mickey D's on the way for breakfast and would be on the beach shortly after the sun peeked over the horizon. We developed entire lists of rules for this outing. One rule was to always take a pair of sandals to wear on the beach sand. This prevented burns on the bottoms of your feet. Another rule was to lather the sunscreen on, preferably SPF twelve million, while in the van on the way to the beach and recoat generously upon arrival. This prevented burn on your exposed skin. We'd spend a couple hours frolicking in the small waves on the shoreline and collect tons of shell fragments and small rocks. We'd be home by noon, before the crowds showed up and before the sun rose high enough to fry small children. When we got home we took naps. Those were great days.

As a surprise we decided to take Frau to Galveston on Mother's Day.

Frau was in a great mood on the drive to Galveston. She told stories about going there with Darling as a little girl, and Darling joined in, adding funny touches that made us laugh. Frau was excited about the adventure. Excitement is contagious and we were all pretty happy to get to the beach.

Strands of seaweed washed up on the beach and the sun cast an ever-strengthening warm radiance on the sandy coastline. Flocks of seagulls whirled and danced overhead, no doubt wanting us to throw food at them. Which we did. Small sand pipers skittered across the sand from wavelet to wavelet, totally ignoring us unless we chased them. Which we did. If you want to see something funny, go ahead and watch a late-forties, overweight pale guy chasing a sand piper across the beach in the sun and laughing like a maniac. I enjoyed myself immensely.

Frau couldn't chase the birds, of course, but she did a good job of coaxing the gulls close to her. We set up a folding lawn chair for her at the edge of the sand, as far from the car as she could manage to walk, far enough so she was on the beach. The only thing brighter than the sun that morning was the smile on Frau's face.

Of course Darling and our teens and I had to wade into the water. We didn't go swimming, which is okay. I am not keen on swimming in the brown waters of Galveston, but there is something innately relaxing about warm waves lapping against your legs and calves.

Darling stayed pretty close to her Mother, but still had a good time. Frau dozed off a few times, then woke up laughing like a little girl at a birthday party, her small hands clapping at the birds as they landed in the sand near her and launched again into the blue sky.

When the day started to get uncomfortable we packed our things and got ready to leave. Beach sand gets everywhere, regardless of what beach you visit. Sand layered our shoes and wedged between our toes and settled in other odd places, then dusted the floorboards of the car as we got in. Frau climbed into the back seat last of all, smiles all over her face.

A man with a sun-burned face and the wrinkled, leathery skin of a perpetual beach comber came over to her as she settled into her seat. Her smile drew him like a bright light draws a moth. He regaled her with a brief story of his unemployment and brought a harmonica to his lips. He played a couple songs, the music joining the cries of the birds and the sounds of the waves striking the beach, blending into a harmony I will never hear again. Frau, of course, gave him some money. He was all set to settle in and provide a concert, but we had to leave.

Frau dozed off again on the way home, perhaps running in the waves in her dreams. Darling helped her to her room when we got home and everyone took showers to remove the ubiquitous sand. Then we took naps.

Galveston beach on Mother's Day remained a happy memory for Frau, and she sparkled whenever she spoke of it. I did too.

On Frau and Generosity

Frau can be surprisingly generous, though I think she might have to work at it. Christmas is a tough time for her. She wavers between giving everyone a dollar (which, by her standards, is a lot of money) and having Darling simply buy them clothes.

One Christmas Frau decided to give her children and grandchildren a certain dollar amount apiece for Christmas. She and Darling made a list. Twelve people total: five children, seven grandchildren. The total amount was a fair chunk of change.

She announced to Darling that she was going to do this, and I absented myself after rolling my eyes. Frau once promised to give one of her grandchildren a hundred dollars to one grandchild for every "A" on her report card. Though I'm sure the promise was meant in good faith, no money changed hands after Frau discovered how many classes the girl had and how often she got report cards. She also told Darling that she wanted to call a radio station and offer one hundred dollars to every child that correctly recited the Ten Commandments. We didn't let her do that, since that could add up. For that matter, I might have called the station for that offer. She also offered to pay tuition for one grandson until she found out what tuition costs. I just left the room. I didn't think Frau would give anyone money for Christmas.

At first Frau tried to figure out how to give each person the money but specify what it was to be spent on. She pondered a trust fund for the grandchildren (all adults at this point, I might add). That became too complicated, so she went to the bank and had them draft twelve cashier's checks. Then she had Darling invite everyone over to the house on the day before New Year's Eve. I was astonished.

Most of them were too busy to come to the house for Christmas. Darling's eldest brother flatly refused; he was too busy. Darling told him he needed to come. He finally agreed and came with his wife. His daughter couldn't make it, but after he discovered his Mother's plan he brought his daughter over on New Year's Day for a few minutes. Then they all came and took Frau out to lunch. And they called every day. For weeks. They were very grateful.

Frau liked being the center of attention, and I am glad for it. I think she liked being generous. I am glad for that also. A generous heart is a hard thing to cultivate.

She still thinks the banks are stealing her money.

A number of years later, just after Christmas, Frau's son M and his wife stopped by to visit. As they talked, the Daughter-In-Law, a sweetheart who spent many, many hours with Frau (and called her "Mom" I might add!) mentioned they were going to the store to buy a new computer. As part of the visit they wanted my opinion on which computer to buy.

As we talked about it, Frau announced that she would buy the computer for her daughter-in-law. Four witnesses, I said loudly, smiling. I was sure the cost would deter Frau and the issue would drop. Darling clearly explained the cost will be over $1600 (an iMac™) and Frau paled a bit, but didn't back down. So in a surprising act of spontaneous generosity, Frau bought her daughter-in-law a computer. I know Frau was pleased because she later pointed at my machine.

"Is this what I bought for her?" she asked me, eyebrows raised slightly.

"Exactly like this one," I replied. Frau grinned broadly and headed back to her room, slowly clapping her chubby little hands. I'd swear she was trying to dance a little jig.

A few days later M comes by and mumbled how he wished his mom would buy him a new computer. I just grinned at that.

On Frau and Cheesecake (and Coffee at Three)

Frau lived with us for many years as her health slowly declined. Darling did her best to keep her mother healthy, but, frankly, it was a losing battle. Darling persevered.

Sometimes the doctors put dietary restrictions on Frau, in an effort to get her to lose weight and improve her blood pressure. Darling cooked meals that were healthy, but her mother's penchant for potatoes interfered in any culinary improvements for Frau's benefit. I no longer cared about the delectable goodies Frau kept in her room, but they certainly weren't helping her get trim and fit. The snacks probably didn't impact her too much, since she needed to keep them in arm's reach of her chair, and her arms were pretty short.

At one point the family Doctor told Frau she needed to avoid chocolate, advice which, surprisingly, Frau heeded. On the next trip to the grocery store I helped bring in a few small bags.

Darling pointed at some bags. "Put one of those boxes in the freezer and the rest can go in the deep freeze."

The bag had cartons of Sarah Lee™ cheesecake. Most of the frozen goodies were strawberry cheesecake, but some were New York Style. They all looked good.

I put a strawberry cheesecake in the freezer and took the rest to the deep freezer. When I got back I helped with the rest of the groceries. "Are we having a party?" It's always nice if I'm informed.

"No," said Darling. "Mom decided she wanted cheesecake with her coffee today."

Thus began a ritual that lasted for years. Every day, almost precisely at three in the afternoon, Darling prepared a slice of cheesecake, still frozen, and a steaming hot cup of instant coffee and took it to her Mom in the Master Suite. If the clock ticked past three in the afternoon Frau would amble out of her room and head toward the kitchen. Darling would then jump up and prepare the cheesecake and coffee.

The cheesecake had to be frozen. When I made a cheesecake, Frau liked it at refrigerator temperature (everyone likes my cheesecakes), but the Sarah Lee™ cheesecakes needed to be left in their frozen state.

Only once did Darling try to warm it a little so Frau could actually cut it with her fork. Frau became angry that Darling ruined it. From then on the cheesecake remained frozen.

When Darling left me to care for her mother, there was always one specific item on my to-do list: cheesecake and coffee for Mom at three. I don't recall ever eating the cheesecake, though Frau offered me some occasionally. I always politely declined.

Eventually the chocolate bars returned and I shrugged. "Let the old woman eat what she wants," I said, when Darling asked me what she should do. "It really isn't going to hurt her."

Darling just smiled and life with her Mother moved forward. Darling cared for her, tiring herself out more and more as the years progressed. Her mother wasn't always in the best of moods, and with some justification. It's hard to be kind and sweet when you are in pain most of the time.

Smiles almost always returned as Darling took her cheesecake and coffee at three.

On Frau and Bon Voyage

In the fall of 2009 I came home from church and found Frau's Son ML and Daughter-in-Law visiting Frau. Frau was unable to stay awake to visit with them, waking and falling asleep over and over again. Darling was deeply concerned about Frau's behavior.

By evening Darling was concerned enough that she wanted Frau to go to the emergency room (ER). Darling couldn't talk her mother into going, though. On the verge of tears Darling called her older brother, asking what she should do. "Whatever you think you need to do," her brother replied. Darling talked to Frau again with no better luck. Tears filled my Darling's eyes.

I went into Frau's room, which everyone knows I do not do, and stood at the side of the bed.

"Hey!" I said. Frau almost opened her eyes and almost looked at me. "You're pretty sick. Darling thinks you need to go to the hospital."

"No, I'm good. God will take care of me." Her eyes drooped closed and her mouth barely moved as she whispered the words.

"Right. I know that. But you can't even open your eyes to talk to me and you're falling asleep constantly. You're sick. If you don't go to the hospital, you're going to die." I'm not usually this blunt, but as I listened to her breathing and looked at Frau's pale face I started to worry.

"No, no. I'm fine. I want to die in my own bed." Oh brother. Darling chimed in that she didn't want her Mom to go just yet, the tears streaming down her face.

I was more direct. "Look, I appreciate that." I spoke loudly so that Frau could hear me and also so she would stay awake long enough to talk to me. "But this isn't a decision that Darling needs to make for you. You decide. You want to stay here in bed, that's fine, but you'll probably die. You want to go, we'll go right now. You know I'm serious or I wouldn't be in your room."

She mumbled something about knowing I only want the best for her, and I wasn't sure if she was serious or sarcastic. I was willing to do what she chose to do. Finally she said "If you think I need to go, then I'll go."

So we went to the ER, wheelchair and oxygen bottles and everything. Darling's brother met us at the hospital. The ER people kicked me out, so I ended up sitting in the waiting room.

Frau stayed in the hospital until Friday when ML brought her home. Darling had a 102 degree fever and bronchitis and could barely breathe.

During the Thanksgiving holiday of 2009 Frau announced that she didn't want to go to the doctor again because he'd put her in the hospital. Which is right, no doubt, and if you heard her trying to breathe you'd put her in the hospital too. Right after Christmas Darling called her brothers to make sure they visited her. Though it didn't look good during the Christmas of 2009, Frau came back home with us.

The trips in and out of the hospital during 2010 exhausted Darling. After two of the hospital visits, Frau needed to go to the rehabilitation center to restore her health, but those visits were incredibly difficult. Darling went to see her and spend time with her almost every day. Those were some tough times, since Frau was convinced (never mind how) that Darling put her into a nursing home, often refusing to believe the doctor sent her to a Rehabilitation Renter.

I actually went a few times, once with my brand-new iPad™ to show Frau. It was the Wi-Fi version, but I still took it to the Rehab Center when we visited. Frau had no problems with it, as opposed to using a mouse and a computer. "Look," I showed her, "when you want to see the next picture, push that one aside and ..."

Unlike the mouse and computer, she picked this one up in a heartbeat. Of course she scanned through my newspaper readers! She wanted to read an article and instinctively touched it. Sure the data was cached, not live, since I didn't have a Wi-Fi connection, but it was good stuff.

After we sat in the Rehab Center for a few hours I fell asleep, my chin on my chest, the television in the room tuned to the local news station. I woke up feeling hot and stuffy, drool on my shirt and my brain clouded with a distinct fuzziness. What do they pipe into that place?

Frau needed to come home as soon as possible. Darling did everything she could to make that happen.

The months after she came back home were tiring and hard on Darling, physically, mentally and emotionally.

In the early part of December, 2010, Frau went back into the hospital with a fever. Again, she had serious trouble breathing. While she was in the hospital she had a silent heart attack. She didn't live to see Christmas of 2010, but died on December 18, in the hospital and surrounded by her three local sons and Darling. I was at the hospital, but I was praying in a different room.

Frau didn't take any of her things with her. None of us do, do we? Eventually, after many months, all her possessions were divided or donated. We donated more than forty large bags of clothes much of it vintage, to a local charity. As it turns out, Frau's forays in the garage sales were also quite fruitful. She had cases of broken jewelry, literally dozens of pounds. Those found different homes.

Frau did, indeed, store a lot of food in her room. Much of it was canned goods, stacked neatly and compactly under her kitchen sinks. She had over a half-dozen cans of sauerkraut, each more than a decade old. I like sauerkraut, but those cans were risky. Canned fruits of indeterminate age were stacked there also, along with various cans of herring and other small fish. Yes, we found candy stuffed in her chair, next to the cushion, squirreled away and forgotten, some of it chocolate. Needless to say, we tossed all the food.

There were many other stories of our years together, some quite angry and many times my fault. Darling had the patience and stamina to take care of her mother for all those years. I didn't. The best I could do was try to take care of Darling.

Some of the other stories were funny, but not really appropriate. There was the single and only time I conscripted the Lass and the Lad to help me clean Frau's room to surprise Darling and lend a helping hand. "No, my Lad, I don't think that brown stuff on the floor is chocolate."

Other memories are tender ones. Frau carefully teaching the Lass to knit, the two of them sitting for hours in Frau's room with knitting needles and laughing. Frau eating at dinner and declaring she never had such a good meal, and what was it, and she never had it before, though we'd eaten the same thing mere weeks earlier. Frau confusing us all by responding to a yes-no question with a firm "No. Ja." That's still something we say now, smiling in remembrance. Frau playing checkers with us and beating us all easily, except for Darling. Frau's explosive exhalation of her cuss phrase "Donnerstag und Freitag" which actually just means "Thursday and Friday" but not in the tones Frau used.

Frau didn't take her suitcase with her either, so carefully packed all those years ago. She doesn't need it though. She's probably running barefoot through fields of Heavenly flowers and laughing.

Darling misses her mother, every day. And, surprisingly, I miss my Frau.

The Present Starts in the Past

Any errors in translations from German to English are entirely mine. I apologize in advance, but tried to maintain at least the essence of the translated documents. Where I deemed appropriate, the documents have names smudged out.

The Present starts in the Past

History records that over six million Jewish people were killed in World War II.

Not as well known is that the Polish people were hated by both the Nazis and the Russian Red Army. Young Hertha, living in the city of Lodz, was right in the middle of that conflict. By the end of World War II over six million of her countrymen would be dead, almost a quarter of the population of Poland.

We don't know much about Hertha's life when she was younger. Born in March of 1925, Hertha was a young girl of 14 when the Germans invaded her home town in Poland. She told us stories that indicated her family was moderately wealthy, with a cook and maid. Instead of walking to church, they had their own carriage with horses. As far as we know, her life continued normally for a few years after the invasion. She told only one story that hints at any direct impact the change of leadership in her home city had on her. Young Hertha saw a Jewish girl about her own age severely beaten by other citizens of Litzmannstadt and she tried to help the girl. Hertha still wept when she told this story, even as an old woman.

We have one photo that shows a young Hertha with her family. Hertha is the child on the left, standing in front of her father.

~ooo~

Hertha had two older sisters. In one story, the eldest got angry with Hertha for not properly beating a rug so the sister made her kneel on a sack of beans for hours as punishment. When their mother saw this, she cried at the older sister's severe discipline.

As a sixteen-year-old girl Hertha noticed a local flour mill with a pond, falling in love with the beauty of the land and the house. They passed this mill on the way to church in their family carriage. For young Hertha this became her fantasy of a perfect place to live.

We know Hertha took a fancy to an older man, a wealthy Master Miller. Born in 1907, Adolf was eighteen years her senior, but she caught his eye. In 1944, when she was only 19, Hertha married Adolf. They moved into his house near his large mill, a pond outside the front door, the very same place that younger Hertha fell in love with two years earlier.

~ooo~

The leaders of Litzmannstadt issued their wedding certificate on August 7, 1944, stamping it with an official seal, which contains the now familiar Nazi swastika. The wedding date was September 2, 1944, though that is not shown on the certificate.

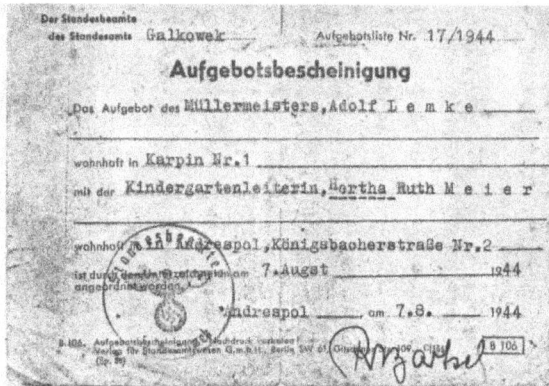

~ooo~

Their marriage certificate, notarized on August 28, 1944 was also issued in Litzmannstadt. It seems the total cost for the marriage certificate was 205.52 German Marks and was based on Adolf's estimated business value of 50,000 German marks.

My Mother-in-law Misadventures

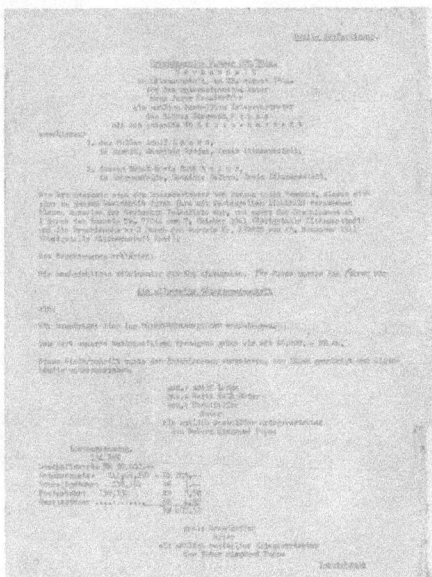

~ooo~

No one told Hertha what to expect from married life. At the time wedding parties lasted an entire week, and the house was full of people, so it was easy for Hertha to hide from her husband for three days after marriage. We have no idea what Adolf thought of that.

Hertha struggled as a young wife with the cooking. The first time she burned the potatoes for dinner, she hurriedly buried them in the back yard. That's the only part of the story we know; she never told us what she fed Adolf or what he thought of his wife's lack of cooking mastery. This wasn't the last time she burned a meal, but it was the only time she buried it (that we know of). She eventually mastered cooking pork chops, sauerkraut, and even potatoes, a staple she had almost every day while living with us.

We have a single wedding photo of the couple.

~ooo~

We don't know how long they had to enjoy their time together before the house became headquarters for a new group of people. The Nazi commander and his men occupied their house and, as Hertha said many times in the following decades, they made her "a servant in her own home."

The Nazis soldiers were not good men and the stories Hertha told of the Nazis in her household were not pleasant. The soldiers shot local people on a whim and fished in the pond with dynamite. They treated Adolf with disdain and more than once attacked him in fits of anger. An ex-soldier in the Polish Army, Adolf refused to join the Nazi army, and this infuriated them. Hertha was a young woman, and that posed an entirely different set of problems.

We have few stories of this time. We do know that at one point some of the other servants overheard the commander and his men plotting to kill Adolf and, eventually, Hertha. That night Adolf and Hertha bundled themselves in as many layers of clothing as they could, took what they could carry and became refugees, fleeing to the part of Germany that was controlled by the Allies. Aside from the few things they could carry, they left everything behind. The once wealthy Master Miller was now a refugee.

Their life in Poland was over forever.

~ooo~

The newly married couple fled with little paperwork. Some of what survived baffles us. We have a doctor's record for Adolf from January, 1944 from the Northwest State Hospital in Litzmannstadt. We have no idea why they saved it. It has the new city name of Litzmannstadt typed over the original city name of Lodz.

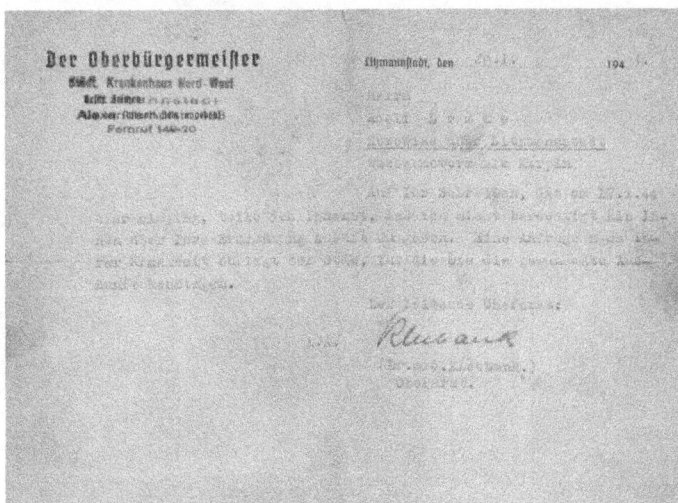

~ooo~

Young Hertha obtained a number of job references before she married Adolf and she kept them. All had glowing praise for her work as a Kindergarten teacher. Both are shown below, one from 1941 and one from 1944, weeks before her marriage.

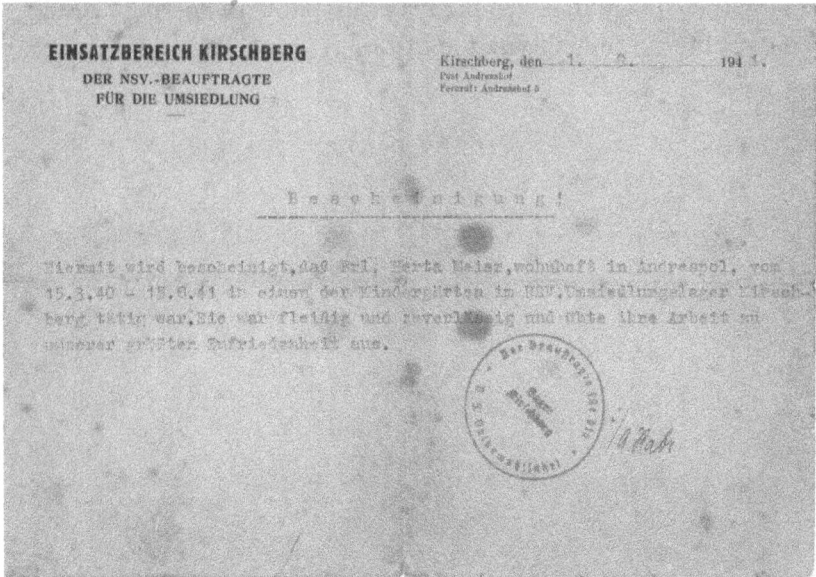

September 1, 1941

Certificate

I hereby certify that Miss Herta, residing in Andrespol, from March 15, 1940 until August 15, 1941 taught in the NSV Kindergarten. She taught in Kirschberg. She was hard-working and reliable and worked to our great satisfaction.

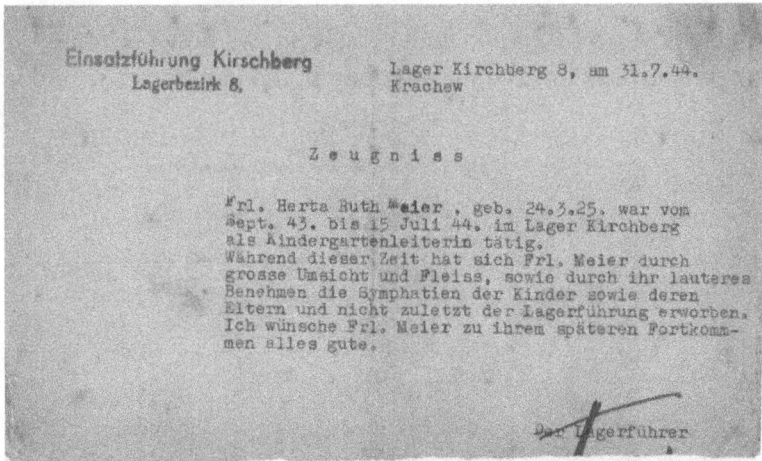

Lager Kirchberg 8, on July 31, 1944

Krachew

Testimony

Miss Herta Ruth, born 3/25/1924 taught from September 1943 until July 15, 1944 in Lager Kirchberg as a head kindergarten teacher.

During this time Miss - gained great respect from children and parents, and not least from the principal for her efforts and skills. I wish her all good in the future.

The Principal

A Bank Book from Litzmannstadt clearly shows how Germany encouraged citizens to save their money in the banks.

Whether you trust a few or thousands of your money, the bank manages your money reliably.
The bank is your friend!

The Passbook (savings book) is a weapon in the struggle for survival of each German citizen and the Nation!

~ooo~

According to history, the Soviet Red Army entered the city of Litzmannstadt (originally called Lodz) on January 18, 1945. Hertha and Adolf still lived there, but we don't recall any stories of the Soviet soldiers, which baffles us. Hertha and Adolf fled their home on April 28, 1946, according to their personally written miniature biographies.

Until they emigrated to the USA they lived in the small city of Gelldorf. Frau only referred to this time as "living in the refugee camps." Though there was not much need for a Master Miller, Adolf was also a skilled carpenter, as well as a capable man with anything mechanical. His sons and daughter inherited his skills.

Hertha's statement

Gelldorf,den 2o. Juni 1951.

Ich,Ehefrau Herta Lemke, besuchte bis zum 15. Lebensjahre die
deutsche Volksschule in Polen. Vom 15.3.1940 bis 15.8.1941 war ich
in einem Kindergarten der NSV, Umsiedlungslager Kirschberg,tätig.
Vom 15.8.1941 ab war ich als Kindergartenleiterin in Andrespol,
Königsbach und Tuschinwald,Kreis Litzmannstadt tätig. Von Sept.1943
bis 15.7.1944 war ich im Lager Kirschberg. Von Juli bis zum 2.9.1944
war ich zu Hause und habe mich am 2.September 1943 verheiratet. Von
diesem Zeitpunkt ab bis April 1946 wohnte ich in Karpin,Kreis Litzmannstadt. Am 28.4.1946 kamen wir als Ostflüchtling in Gelldorf
Kreis Schaumburg-Lippe an,wo wir auch jetzt noch wohnen.

Gelldorf, on June 20, 1951

*I, Hertha, a housewife, attended the German elementary school in
Poland until I was fifteen. From March 15, 1940 until August 15, 1941
I taught in the NSV Kindergarten in Kirschberg. From August 15,
1941 I was a Head Kindergarten teacher in Adrespol, Konigsbach and
Tuschinwald near the city of Litzmannstadt. From September, 1943
until July 15, 1944 I was in Camp Kirschberg. From July until
September 2, 1944 I stayed at home and was married on September 2,
1944. From that date until April 1946 I lived in Karpin, Litzmannstadt.
On April 28, 1946 we arrived as refugees in Gelldorf district of
Schaumburg-Lippe, where we now live.*

~ooo~

Adolf's statement

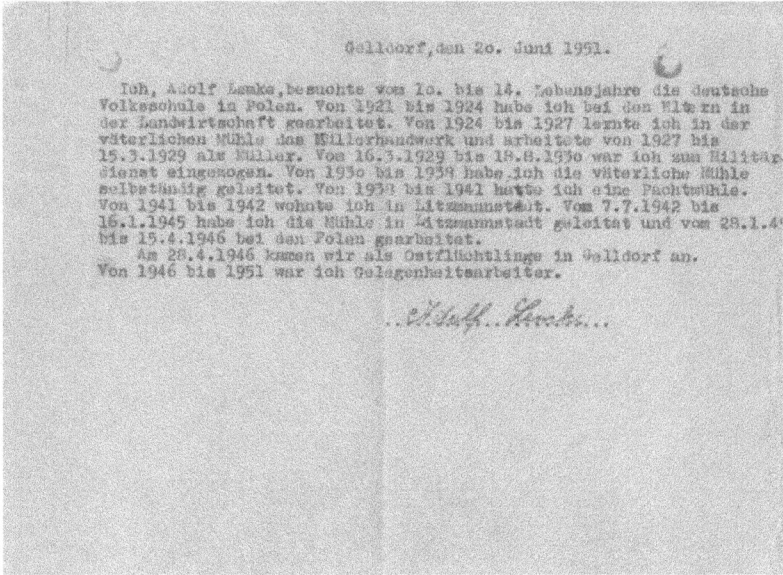

Gelldorf, on June 20, 1951

I, Adolf, attended the German elementary school in Poland until I was fourteen. From 1921 to 1924 I worked with my parents in agriculture. From 1924 to 1927 I learned the Miller craft in my Father's mill and worked from 1927 until March 15, 1929 as a Miller. From March 16, 1929 until August 18, 1930 I was drafted for military service. From 1930 until 1938 I was in charge of my Father's mill. From 1938 until 1941 I leased a mill. From 1941 until 1942 I lived in Litzmannstadt. From July 7, 1942 until January 16, 1945 I supervised the mill in Litzmannstadt and worked from January 28, 1945 until April 15, 1946 for the Polish. On April 28, 1946 we came as refugees to Gelldorf. From 1946 until 1951 I was a casual laborer.

~ooo~

We have a single picture of Hertha in Gelldorf, perhaps the late 1940s or early 1950s. Hertha signed the back of it with "I love you" in English. Darling says this might be around the time that Hertha's mother died, which could explain her sad expression.

~ooo~

The family obtained "Proof of Residence" papers on September, 1951 from the Mayor of Gelldorf. Within the document the Mayor stated "*I hereby certify that the above mentioned persons have resided continuously in the Western zones of Germany since April 28, 1946.*" We think this paved the way for them to obtain German Passports.

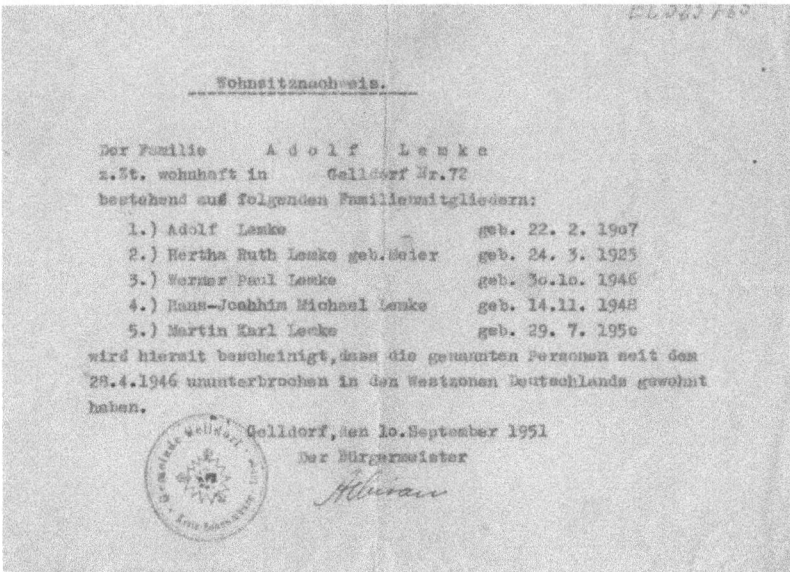

~ooo~

Young Hertha took classes in English and USA orientation in 1952.

~ooo~

We have a picture of two of the boys, taken in Germany sometime probably in the very early 1950s.

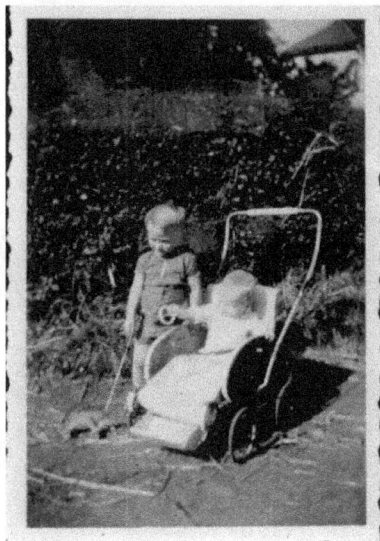

~ooo~

We have a picture of all three boys, probably taken while they still lived in Germany.

In the early 1950s a small church community in Texas paid for Adolf, Hertha and their three sons to come to Texas. For a few years they lived in a small town north of the city of Houston. We have a photo of Hertha, her four boys and Darling.

~ooo~

Frau and her husband became US citizens on July 29th, 1957. Frau
was extremely proud of her American citizenship. When Senator John.
F. Kennedy ran for President, Hertha sent him a telegram to express
her conditional backing. We were surprised to find it among her
papers.

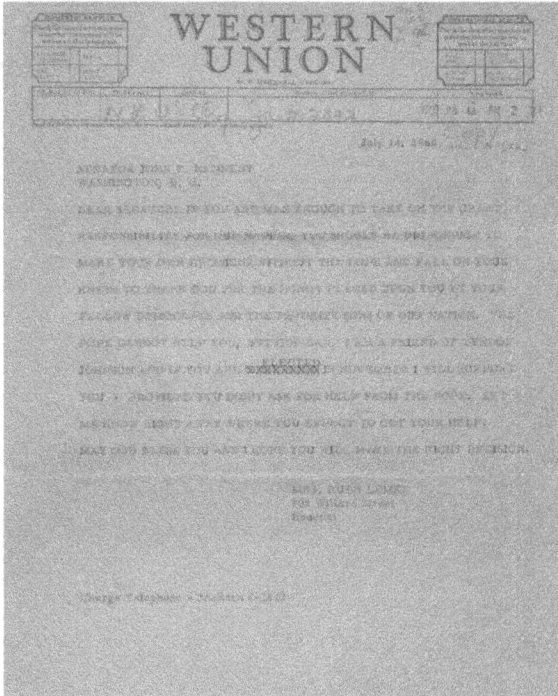

July 14, 1960

Senator John F. Kennedy

Washington, D.C.

Dear Senator: If you are man enough to take on the great responsibility
for our nation, you should be big enough to make your own decisions
without the Pope and fall on your knees to thank God for the honor
placed upon you by your fellow Democrats and the favorite sons of

our Nation. The Pope cannot help you, but God can. I am a friend of Lyndon Johnson and if you are elected in November I will support you - provided you don't ask for help from the Pope. Let me know right away where you expect to get your help. May God bless you and I hope you will make the right decision.

~ooo~

Hertha visited her family in Oberkirche, Germany in 1968, her last visit to see her father while he was still living. Hertha is the young lady wearing the necklace. The man seated on the far right is her father.

My Mother-in-law Misadventures

My favorite picture from Hertha's early years shows the simple joy of Mother and child, a picture of Hertha and a very young Darling. That is all I need to know of young Hertha. I met Frau many decades later after Darling captured my heart.

###

Thank you for reading my book. I hope you enjoyed these stories. I usually write fiction, but these were stories that I wanted to share. May your journey through life be joyful.

Also from Undefined Logic, LLC

Our other book, Preparing for the Fiscal Cliff still contains a lot of useful information. The US government never really addressed that Fiscal Cliff issue did they? You might want to take a look at the book and see what you can do to help your family in the coming years.

We also have a few apps for the iPhone and a few for the Droid. We plan to develop more, and refresh the ones we have. Check us out at our website www.undefinedlogic.mobi

Connect with Vince Online:

My blog: http://www.o-dark-thirty.blogspot.com/

All the photos in this book are available in an album on my Facebook account at www.facebook.com/vincent.bernhardt.56
My twitter name is @vbbernhardt. I don't tweet much, though.